Low-Budget Marketing
for ROOKIES

Titles in the *for* ROOKIES series

About the author

Following almost a decade in the marketing industry in the UK and Australia, **Karen McCreadie** decided to combine her knowledge of marketing and passion for writing to help professionals to create the ultimate marketing and business development tool – a book! Good marketing is all about getting the customer's attention and inspiring action – few marketing initiatives do that as well as a content-rich, well-written book. A book develops a personal brand, establishes the author as an expert, protects IP, increases revenue and offers business professionals a unique way to create a competitive advantage in an increasingly crowded marketplace.

In her capacity as marketer and ghostwriter, Karen writes for CEOs, business coaches, consultants, international speakers, professional services personnel and entrepreneurs who don't necessarily have the time or inclination to spend hours translating their ideas into a polished product. For more information, please visit www.wordarchitect.com.

Low-Budget Marketing
for ROOKIES

Copyright © 2009 LID Editorial Empresarial and Marshall Cavendish Limited

First published in 2009 by

Marshall Cavendish Limited
Fifth Floor
32–38 Saffron Hill
London EC1N 8FH
United Kingdom
T: +44 (0)20 7421 8120
F: +44 (0)20 7421 8121
sales@marshallcavendish.co.uk
www.marshallcavendish.co.uk

A member of **BPR**
businesspublishersroundtable.com

Marshall Cavendish is a trademark of Times Publishing Limited

Other Marshall Cavendish offices: Marshall Cavendish International (Asia) Private
Limited, 1 New Industrial Road, Singapore 536196 • Marshall Cavendish Corporation.
99 White Plains Road, Tarrytown NY 10591–9001, USA • Marshall Cavendish International
(Thailand) Co Ltd. 253 Asoke, 12th Floor, Sukhumvit 21 Road, Klongtoey Nua, Wattana,
Bangkok 10110, Thailand • Marshall Cavendish (Malaysia) Sdn Bhd, Times Subang, Lot 46,
Subang Hi-Tech Industrial Park, Batu Tiga, 40000 Shah Alam, Selangor Darul Ehsan,
Malaysia

The author and publisher have used their best efforts in preparing this book and disclaim
liability arising directly and indirectly from the use and application of this book.

All reasonable efforts have been made to obtain necessary copyright permissions. Any
omissions or errors are unintentional and will, if brought to the attention of the publisher,
be corrected in future printings.

A CIP record for this book is available from the British Library

ISBN 978-0-462-09957-6

Illustrations by Nuria Aparicio and Joan Guardiet

Printed and bound in Great Britain by
TJ International Limited, Padstow, Cornwall

Contents

Introduction

"Marketing is an attitude, not a department"
– Phil Wexter

All too often marketing is seen as a subject shrouded in mystery, a mercurial and elusive profession populated by snake-oil salesmen adept in the art of smoke and mirrors. As a result it's an area of small business that is all too often neglected. People are put off by the jargon and the perception that there are some secrets to good marketing that only the chosen few have access to. They assume that good marketing involves infectious TV campaigns, innovative direct marketing and celebrity endorsements. Visions of pin-striped ad-men with budgets to rival the national debt reinforce the illusion that good marketing is for the "big boys" and must therefore cost a fortune.

As a result it just doesn't get done.

Whether you find yourself in a position where your boss has asked you to take on some marketing responsibilities or whether you are a small business owner who recognizes the importance of marketing but just don't know where to begin – this book will help. Often confusion

8 about what to do and where to start can make marketing a daunting prospect and so we sweep it under the carpet for another day. Ironically when that day finally arrives it invariably does so because marketing has been systematically ignored and as a result sales are down and cash flow is under pressure.

But don't despair – you don't need bottomless pockets, you just need to avoid the typical mistakes and get the basics right.

The mistakes people make when it comes to marketing are universal:

- They don't know their customers and therefore have no way of distinguishing between a good customer and a bad one.
- They get overly attached to their product or service and can't see it from the customer's perspective.
- They don't know their target market or understand why people buy their product or service, and therefore don't know who to target to maximize their marketing success.
- They engage in DIY marketing that looks more like a school project than the face of a professional business and consequently gives the wrong impression. (Perception is everything in business – you must look the part, even if you are working out of the spare bedroom!)
- They don't hold information about past and present customers.
- They don't follow up and stay in communication with their customers.
- They don't have a website, or if they do it screams "amateur" and is invariably not optimized for search engines.
- They don't differentiate.

Nowhere on that list do you see "They don't have a million pound budget." Contrary to popular belief, marketing isn't really that complicated, and it certainly doesn't have to break the bank. Think of it like baking a cake. The ingredients to make a delicious cake are very basic – flour, butter, sugar and maybe an egg or two. If you're feeling frisky you could add some cocoa powder. But even with the chocolate addition, none of the ingredients are rare, extravagant or expensive – they can be bought from any corner shop for a few coins.

Get those ingredients wrong, however, and no amount of decoration is going to hide the error. Marketing is the same – if you get the basics wrong, the cake ain't going to bake! Much of the professional advertising and marketing that people assume is "proper marketing" is actually just decoration. Some of it has been extremely successful, and powerful brands have been forged through innovative and exciting campaigns. But if you had the sort of money you need for that kind of campaign, you wouldn't be reading this book, would you?

Getting the basics right is what this book is all about. And if you do that, then you will see a radical change in your bottom line.

There are only five ways to make money in business:

1. Sell to more customers.
2. Sell more often to customers.
3. Increase your price.
4. Cut expenses.
5. Create an asset and sell it.

Marketing is involved in four out of five of those money-making opportunities, so it's not something you can ignore. Good marketing sells more products, good marketing sells more products more often, and good marketing can even convince your customers of the merits of a price increase. (Just remember Stella Artois – reassuringly expensive!) And finally, good marketing can make your business a more viable asset, so it needs to be viewed as an important investment rather than an expense to be minimized.

Forget wordy definitions in dry academic tomes; quite simply, marketing is everything your company does, seen from your customers' perspective. Every time your customer or potential customer comes into contact with your company there is a marketing opportunity, and that contact will either positively or negatively influence your chance of a sale. The medium of that communication can be everything from newspaper advertising to direct mail to your website

10

– even how you handle complaints and how your receptionist answers the phone.

You and your staff need to adopt a marketing attitude; you have to constantly be prepared to step into your customers' shoes and ensure that their experience of your product, service and business is second to none.

So forget big budget, think simple, practical and accessible – that's what this little book is all about. It won't bore you to death with text-book definitions and outdated formulas and I promise to keep the jargon to an absolute minimum. The ideas don't need you to invest much money – all they need is your time. Don't get overwhelmed by the task ahead, but read the book from cover to cover and then choose a couple of things to get you started. Marketing is like eating an elephant; it's best to take little manageable bites, and don't look up at what you're tackling! What I'm suggesting isn't always easy, and it demands your attention and determination, but that's why so few people do it. There's nothing mystical about the suggestions I offer, but the results can be magical.

Notes

Before we plunge into specific aspects of marketing, it's important to understand the psychology of human behaviour and the underlying philosophy of marketing. If we gain an appreciation for why people do the things they do, then you can apply those insights to your marketing to make it more effective. After all, if you know what bases to cover and what buttons to press to get a "yes" you'll improve your results, regardless of the medium you use.

CHAPTER 1

Psychology and philosophy of marketing

The psychology of persuasion

In his book *Influence: Science and Practice*, Robert B. Cialdini talks about the six basic principles of psychology that direct human behaviour. His work is the result of extensive experimental studies on the "weapons of influence", together with three years of immersion in the world of compliance professionals – salespeople, fundraisers, advertisers and others. Cialdini wanted to understand what persuaded people to say "Yes".

The implications of Cialdini's work are profound. By identifying these six principles he has demystified brilliant sales and marketing. And in doing so he has given us the tools to exponentially improve our results. By understanding the unconscious forces that are at work in human psychology we can learn how to tap into them in the promotion of our own business and guard ourselves against their unscrupulous application. Knowing about these principles makes manipulation much easier, but be warned – marketing without integrity is simply a waste of time and money. People will not be fooled twice and businesses don't survive by selling something they can't consistently deliver.

14   Once you understand why you are influenced to act in certain situations, then you can apply that knowledge to all sorts of areas of your life, whether you are trying to encourage your customers to buy your product or whether you'd just like your partner to fix the leaking tap in the laundry or make your favourite cheesecake!

Rookie Buster

Marketing without integrity is simply a waste of time and money.

According to Cialdini's research findings, the six basic principles of psychology that direct human behaviour are:

- Reciprocation.
- Consistency.
- Social proof.
- Liking.
- Authority.
- Scarcity.

Reciprocation

Essentially the law of reciprocity is the innate desire to redress the balance. Test it for yourself and send Christmas cards to a random selection of perfect strangers. According to Cialdini, a university professor did just that and was flooded with return cards, most of which didn't even inquire about his identity. Reciprocation explains this, because when we are given something, we feel the need to give something back. It works in all relationships and across all cultures. If you have a friendship and you seem to consistently give more to that friendship than you receive, sooner or later the friendship will dissolve because there was no reciprocity.

Cialdini points to the Hare Krishna Society to illustrate the power of reciprocity in action. Before the 1970s, the Hare Krishna was a fairly obscure organization. Their fundraising tactic was to approach people in the street and ask for money, but Krishna devotees looked out of place in just about any setting and they were not usually warmly received. But then there was a remarkable growth in Krishna numbers and wealth, and it was all down to reciprocity. Before being asked for a donation the potential donor was given a "gift" – either a book or magazine, or (the most cost-effective version) just a flower. The receiver of the gift felt an internal compulsion to reciprocate with a donation. Even if they didn't want the flower or tried to return the book or magazine, they still gave a donation. Fundraising went through the roof.

This principle is used widely in marketing in the form of "free gifts" and membership offers. By offering a sample of your product or service to a potential customer without obligation you are giving them something of value (either real or perceived) that activates the law of reciprocity. This imbalance makes the sale easier because of the customer's desire to balance the books!

Rookie Buster

By offering a sample of your product or service to a potential customer without obligation you are giving them something of value (either real or perceived) that activates the law of reciprocity.

Consistency

The strongest force in the human personality is the need to remain consistent with the identity we project to the world. What this means is that we have an obsessive desire to be (or appear to be) consistent. Once we make a choice or take a stand we will encounter personal and interpersonal pressures to behave consistently with that commitment.

16

It is this force that causes people to stick to a poor business strategy or stay in an abusive relationship. This internal driver is powerful enough to cause us to stay in situations or act in certain ways that are quite clearly not in our best interests. And often we will know that, but continue anyway!

Why is this important in marketing? It is one of the factors that explain why it is so much harder to gain a new customer than it is to keep an existing one. Once someone makes a choice to do business, the drive for consistency starts to take effect. Basically we want to be right! No one likes to make decisions and choices that turn out to be wrong. Instead we want to feel comforted and happy with those choices. Initially consistency is tentative in the buying relationship, but this is why loyalty programmes work – because once someone has become a customer and bought several times, there is a strong unconscious desire to maintain that relationship. Even to the point at which the customer will forgive errors because they don't want to believe their decision to get involved in the first place was a mistake!

Rookie Buster

Once someone has become a customer and bought several times, there is a strong unconscious desire to maintain that relationship.

Social proof

This principle relates to the comfort and acceptance generated by the herd, and it particularly influences what constitutes correct behaviour. We decide whether our behaviour is correct to the degree that we see others like us performing that behaviour. This innate drive works well in most situations and can help us to avoid offending other people, especially in different cultures. However, it's open to abuse because it short-circuits our decision-making. Instead of making up our own minds, we look around us to see what others are doing and then proceed without any real, conscious engagement in the situation. We behave like sheep.

Again marketers and sales people have found ways to tap into this. Social proof is why testimonials work; they reassure us that other people who are like us have made the buying decision and it has been successful. The assumption is, "If you are happy with your choice to buy that product and you're like me, then I will be happy with the product too."

Liking

Life is all about relationships. And relationships, whether personal or professional, stand a far higher chance of long-term success if the two parties like each other. We do business with people we like. The famous trial attorney Clarence Darrow once said, "The true job of a trial attorney is to get the jury to like their client." In fact in most courtroom situations the jury will make an initial evaluation and decision as to the guilt or innocence of the defendant within the first five minutes. All the information that comes in after that point will go to substantiate the decision they have already made. The jurors will actually ignore information that does not "agree" with their initial assessment – thus conforming to Cialdini's earlier principle of consistency. If they have chosen "guilty" in those first critical minutes, there will be a strong desire to remain consistent with that initial choice.

The principle of liking is self-evident when you consider that often the best sales people are likeable individuals. They are friendly and warm and put potential customers at ease. The sales process is not a series of steps and tricks; it's just a conversation. As a result, good salespeople can make sales look effortless.

18   Authority

This principle illustrates just how powerfully influenced we are by authority – either real or perceived. We are extremely susceptible to requests that are made by people in positions of authority. We automatically trust these individuals, such as the doctor in his crisp white coat, whether that trust is warranted or not. Just how much power we hand over, based on assumption of authority, was alarmingly demonstrated by the Milgram experiments. An official researcher presided over an experiment where participant A had to administer electric shocks to participant B. The researcher systematically told A to increase the shock voltage until B was screaming and begging them to stop. Often A was also deeply distraught and pleading with the researcher to allow them to stop, and yet when pressed to continue usually did. There was in fact no electric shock, and B was only pretending to be in pain for the sake of the experiment, but it demonstrated very conclusively just how powerful authority can be. And just how far we are prepared to go at the request of an authority figure!

Rookie Buster

The sales process is not a series of steps and tricks; it's just a conversation.

Marketers have used this to great effect by getting celebrity endorsements or testimonials from either perceived or real experts in the field. For example, health supplements may be endorsed by a famous athlete and accompanied by a testimonial from a leading nutritionist.

Scarcity

The principle of scarcity refers to the fact that opportunities seem more valuable to us when they are less available. Cialdini refers to his own experience of this principle in action when a Mormon temple near where he lived was being refurbished. He had never had any desire to visit the temple until he read an article that talked about a special inner sanctum of the temple to which no one but high-ranking church members had access. There was, however, one exception to the rule. For a few days after the temple was constructed, non-members were allowed to tour the entire building. The recent renovations had been extensive enough to warrant such a tour. Cialdini found himself suddenly very interested in visiting – even though he had never had any previous desire to do so. The idea that it was a fleeting opportunity made it unconsciously appealing, albeit consciously confusing!

Rookie Buster

Opportunities seem more valuable to us when they are less available.

Open any magazine and you will see "Limited Offer – must close Sunday Xth September" or "Limited edition collector's item – only 7 left". This feeling that we may miss out on something special and unique will influence us to take action. Even when we know it's probably a marketing trick!

By understanding how these six psychological factors work you stand a better chance of meeting your customers' needs and improving your success rate. Now let's look at the philosophy of marketing.

20 *Philosophy*

David Ogilvy, one of the greatest advertising gurus of all time, said, "People don't buy products, they buy solutions." Harvard marketing professor Theodore Levitt expressed the same concept when he said, "People don't want to buy a quarter-inch drill. They want a quarter-inch hole!"

Rookie Buster

People don't buy products, they buy solutions.

Every product or service is the solution to a real or perceived problem. If I live in a rural part of the country where public transport is limited, then I have a transportation and time management problem. Buying a car is my solution.

Consumerism is built on the identification of problems, so that business can solve them and make money. The pharmaceutical industry is particularly adept at this as they come up with new conditions, disorders and syndromes that willing hypochondriacs will spend good money to treat.

Personally I don't agree with how far some industries and businesses go in this process, but the fact is that they do it because it works. If you are in business, the first thing you need to do is get very clear about the problems your product or service solves.

The simplest and most useful philosophy I've ever come across is:

PROBLEM ➜ AGGRAVATE ➜ SOLVE

And that means that you have to know what problem your potential customers have or could have in order for them to consider spending their hard earned cash on your product or service.

Coach's notes

Think about your business and write down three problems that your product or service solves:

1. ....

2. ....

3. ....

This is the PROBLEM phase.

For each problem, write down a consequence of that problem *not* being solved, and focus on how the customer might feel if they don't take action.

1. ....

2. ....

3. ....

This is the AGGRAVATION phase.

For each problem, write down the consequence of that problem if it *is* solved, and focus on the benefits the person will experience and how they might feel if they do take action.

1. ....

2. ....

3. ....

This is the SOLVE phase.

For example, I am a freelance writer. I write everything from websites to articles to ghostwriting books. So what problem does a potential customer have if they are searching for a ghostwriter?

1. A time problem. Many of the people I work with are busy professionals, international speakers or business owners who simply don't have the time to write a book. As a result, "Write my book" has been on their New Year's Resolution list for years, and it haunts them!

2. An ability problem. Often some of those individuals readily admit that writing is not a natural strength, and yet they are confident their ideas are worth writing about. They recognize therefore they need someone to help get those ideas out of their head and on to paper.

3. A business or product development problem. In many cases, especially for consultants or speakers, a book acts as a powerful business card. Being an "author" adds weight and kudos to an individual and often allows them to generate more business or increase their fees. For speakers a book can be sold at the back of presentations and generate additional revenue.

The consequences and feelings of *not solving* those problems are:

1. They never get the book they have always dreamed of writing, because every time they sit down to write it something happens that needs their attention. Each New Year they add "Write my book" to their annual goals and feel despondent. It becomes like a weight around their neck until finally either someone beats them to it and writes the book they were going to write, or it just falls by the wayside. It becomes a source of regret and sadness.

2. They never get the quality of book they envisaged in their mind. The translation from mind to page is clunky and disappointing. The person realizes that not only have they been haunted for years until they finally wrote it, but now that they have written it, it's actually not very good and doesn't do justice to their ideas and theories.

3. They lose money and potential new business. They also miss out on wider recognition and acknowledgement in their field.

The consequences and feelings of *solving* those problems are:

1. The client is able to get on with their day-to-day activity without worrying about how to find the time to write their

book. They are able to focus all their time and energy on other important aspects of their business or life. That brings a feeling a relief because they know their dream is progressing without their constant involvement.

2. Because I ensure I write in the individual's own style, not my own, they feel comforted that their book still sounds like them. They recognize themselves in the pages and are excited to see it come together. In the meantime they are able to do what *they* do best. Writing is not a skill everyone naturally has, and for many the acceptance and acknowledgement of that is liberating.

3. They make more money. People who can add "author" to their resumé attract attention. Whether it's justified or not, being an author elevates you to "expert" status faster than anything else known to mankind, and experts can charge more. For those in the seminar industry, having a book is essential PR and provides lucrative "back of the room" product sales.

Once you have identified at least three problems (or more if you can find them) and worked through the three stages, then you simply incorporate those elements into your marketing. You want people to recognize themselves and their own situation in your communication. If someone resonates with your message and feels that you truly understand their "unique" problem, then you are in a far better position to be the solution they eventually choose.

To help you think about what problems your product or service might solve, use the 4R formula. This simple formula comes from a quirky little book called *The Lazy Man's Way to Riches* by Joe Karbo. Karbo reminds us that "No man can get rich unless he enriches others. And that enrichment can and does consist of making another's life easier, or simpler, or more fulfilling."

Karbo suggests we always remember the Four Rs:

Reincarnation
We want to matter; we want to feel that our time in life has been useful and that we have left our mark. We want to create something that will in some way live on after we are no longer around. So how can your product or service help someone leave his or her mark?

Recognition
We want to feel respected and admired by others. We want to be recognized and appreciated for our efforts. How can your product or service help someone feel important and valued?

Romance
Sex sells! But even after the burning passion has died down, everyone wants to feel wanted, loved and cared for. How does your product or service help someone to feel more attractive, desirable or popular? How does it make them feel good about themselves?

Reward
Reward can take many forms, such as feeling safer, healthier and happier, or the opportunity to make or save more money. We want to know that the purchase will reward us in some way. What will the reward be for buying your product or service?

Not all the Rs will be relevant to every product, but using them might help you think about your offering a little differently.

Go for it! Marketing is not about tricking people into buying your product – it's about understanding why people buy, so that you can position your offering in a way that will resonate with your market. It's about working out what problem you solve, and making that proposition clear in everything you do. Start that process today by brainstorming with your staff. Use the Problem Identification section in the Coach's Notes exercise above and see what you discover.

26 Notes

Notes

Socrates was right when he said "Know thyself." If he was a marketer he would have taken the idea two steps further to include "Know thy customer" and "Know thy market." When you are thoroughly familiar with your customers and the market you compete in, then you can find your niche and prosper, regardless of the economy or the competition.

CHAPTER 2

Target marketing and finding your niche

Who is your audience?

If you're reading this book chances are that you are already in business. Perhaps you are a business owner frustrated at the lack of sales, or perhaps you are the employee in search of some cost-effective ideas to increase revenue. Or maybe you're a sole trader looking for some ideas to generate new business. Whatever your situation, know one thing – shotgun marketing is expensive and wasteful, two unsavoury elements to any marketing campaign, especially for the cash-strapped small business. Unless you have an enormous budget, it's not possible to compete in a generic marketplace and hope your shotgun approach might wing a few prospects on the way down! It's all about market segmentation. So forget chasing a small slice of a gigantic pie and instead focus on a larger slice of a much more manageable pie. Put away that shotgun and learn how to hit the bull's-eye with a rifle.

And if you want to hit bull's-eye you have to know what target you're aiming for in the first place…

30 *Why is it important to know your customers?*

Quite simply because it puts you in charge!

For a start, not all customers are created equal. You may have heard of the Pareto Principle (otherwise known as the 80/20 rule). This rule states that 80 per cent of your revenue comes from 20 per cent of your customers. You need to know who those 20 per cent are!

Rookie Buster

Forget chasing a small slice of a gigantic pie and instead focus on a larger slice of a much more manageable pie.

In business we often respond to the squeakiest wheel. The customers that make the most noise get the most attention, but unless those noisy and demanding customers are in that 20 per cent and financially validate that extra support, then you are wasting valuable time and effort on the wrong people. Let them go to the competition! Let your competition waste time and effort keeping them happy. You need to focus on making sure that your best customers are super happy and that you're bending over backwards for *them*, not for someone who spends £8 every two years and expects you to drop everything when they call!

If you know who your best customers are, you can do two things. First you can circulate their names to everyone in your business to ensure they are always given priority. And secondly, if you know who they are, you can create a customer profile that may allow you to identify ways to reach other people like them and/or target niche groups within the larger generic market.

On top of that, if you know about your customers, then you can work out how useful your marketing efforts are by calculating their marginal net worth. Say for example you run a marketing campaign

and you entice 56 new customers into your business at an average loss   31
per customer of £10 (calculated as total marketing cost minus sales
generated divided by number of new customers). On the face of it that
may look like a poor campaign, but you need to look at the lifetime
value of those new customers. If you know from your customer analysis that your average customer spends £150 a year and stays for 5 years,
then the lifetime value of that customer is £740 (£150 × 5 – £10 initial
loss). And that doesn't take into consideration any dedicated efforts to
up-sell, cross-sell or increase their frequency of purchase (more on all
this in Chapter 5.)

Developing a customer profile

Finding out about your customers isn't always easy – especially if you
don't have a central database that has recorded at least some of the basic
data. But all the information you need does already exist in your business, it's not "missing". Go and find it – even if that means sifting through
files in your sales, accounts or customer services departments.

At the very least create a spreadsheet of the data you collect – that
way, when you do eventually get that all-important database you will
be able to import large chunks of information for later use. For the
record, you should also be collecting the names and addresses of
people who have requested information from you but have perhaps
not bought yet, such as the people who hand in their business cards at
industry events, or entrants into any competitions you have run. You
should be collecting the names and addresses of anyone who has had
any contact with you in the past. These people at least know who you
are and could, with the right offer and incentive, be persuaded to buy.

Rookie Buster

You should be collecting the names and addresses of
anyone who has had any contact with you in the past.

But let's concentrate on actual customers just now. If you have thousands of customers and seriously don't know where to start, then ask the people already in your business for their advice. Remember you are trying to work out who your best clients are so that you can see if they share any common characteristics *and* so that you can ensure you really look after them. Your accounts receivable staff, sales force and dispatch personnel will probably each be able to give you ten names of people they deal with on a regular basis.

Once you have some names and have verified their relative importance to your business, call them up and invite them to lunch – at your expense. If a face-to-face meeting isn't possible, then arrange a good time to call for a chat. Prepare some questions and have a conversation. Explain what you are trying to do. Tell them how much you value their business and that you would like to ask them a few questions to see if there is any way you can improve their experience. Find out what problems you solve for them, why they are loyal, what magazines they read, what influences them to buy from you. Are they that interested in the price, or is it something else? Do they have any insights or suggestions to share with you? Do they enjoy the working relationship with a particular member of your staff? Do they attend any industry events or subscribe to any industry-specific magazines? You are simply trying to build up a better picture of who this person is and why he or she buys from you. And make sure you acknowledge their input by sending them a thank-you gift.

Basic factors to think about…

- Geographic.
- Demographic.
- Psychographic.

Geographic considerations are straightforward – where are your best customers physically located? Is most of your business located within a few miles from home?

Demographics is concerned with the statistical characteristics of

your market, such as age, income, sex, marital status, number of children, occupation and social class, etc. Are there are demographic clus-
ters within your customer base?

And finally psychographics – this is where the real difference is
made in terms of targeting. If you can uncover the psychographic
characteristics of your target market, you can tailor your message to
gain empathy and ensure your audience engages with the message
long enough to make a sale. Psychographics identifies the type of
person that buys in terms of their lifestyle and personality.

Your goal is to build a customer profile for your best customers –
the 20 per cent that account for 80 per cent of your revenue. If possible
you should also look at your average customer across the entire business and find out whether there are similarities in the bottom 20 per
cent of your customer base. The reason is simple – if you discover that
your bottom 20 per cent responded to an advert placed in a particular
magazine, then why would you continue marketing in that way?
Remember, not all customers are created equal. Find out who is profitable and who you and your team enjoy working with – and go find
more of *those* people.

Rookie Buster

Your goal is to build a customer profile for your best
customers – the 20 per cent that account for 80 per cent of
your revenue.

If you know the information about individual customers, you can
then establish a customer profile of who your best, worst and average
customer is.

Ideally you should have a good contact database that will give you
that information automatically. Most good contact databases have a
LTV (Life Time Value) or RFM (Recency, Frequency, Monetary value)
feature, which will display a score to indicate the relative merits of each

34 customer. This score, assigned to each contact, is automatically calculated from an algorithm based on the weighted importance of how often a customer buys, how much they spend and how long they stay.

Know your market

The biggest mistake you can make is to fall in love with a product or service. Don't rush out to make a prototype or (worse) rush it into production without any thought for who might actually want it. I remember meeting a would-be public speaker many years ago who had such confidence in his business venture that he sank everything he had into the creation of 10,000 sets of CDs and workbooks. At the time, however, he had only a handful of clients and was as yet untested in the speaking arena. I don't know what happened to those 10,000 units, but I'm guessing they are still in the garage. *Never* go to market without testing first.

Getting this wrong can be disastrous for your business, even if it does make for good television.

Rookie Buster

Never go to market without testing first.

Watching would-be entrepreneurs pitch their ideas to the panel of successful business people in the TV show *Dragons' Den* can be heart wrenching. I remember one man who had developed a backpack device that meant that his movements were mimicked by an animated character on a screen in front of him. There was no denying it was quite brilliant, but who on earth would buy it? There was absolutely no

market for his product, and yet this man had invested years and heaven   35
knows how much money in its development. He had fallen in love
with his product, and that can be fatal.

Or what about another TV show, *The Apprentice*? In this show,
which sees ambitious and often obnoxious wannabe high flyers
compete for a job with Sir Alan Sugar, the idea of target marketing can
be hysterical. In the fourth series, one of the self-professed sales gurus
was charged with renting out a Ferrari F360. And believe it or not he
took this top-of-the-range sports car to the vegetable section of Porto-
bello Road market in London! First you have to know there is a market
for your product, and secondly you have to go where that target market
is!

How to find out about your market?

One of the quickest and easiest ways to know what's going on in your
industry is to assess your competition. Pay attention to what your
competitors are doing. Focus on your top three rivals plus the one
business that is doing badly in your sector.

- Get on their mailing list – what direct mail are they sending?
  What offers are they making to their customer base?
- Buy a product from them and see how efficiently they deliver –
  are there any chinks in their armour?
- Read industry magazines.
- Attend industry events.
- Scan the local press for their adverts. What offers are they
  making? While you may not be sure how effective their
  advertising is, you can gauge how much marketing activity they
  are doing. Chances are the ones that are successful are keeping
  themselves in the public eye through a variety of channels. You
  need to know what those channels are.
- Collect their brochures and get their annual report. Do they
  mention their marketing efforts or budget? Can you glean any
  information about their sales strategy?
- Visit their website frequently.

36 Success (and failure) leaves clues, and it's your job to decipher those clues when it comes to your competition – who is doing well, who is doing badly, and what can you emulate and improve upon to put yourself ahead.

Rookie Buster

Pay attention to what your competitors are doing.

The legendary copywriter Gary Halbert tells a simple story about getting your targeting right. He once asked a crowd in one of his seminars what they thought they would need in order to create a successful hot dog stand. In true seminar style the audience shouted out various answers:

- "Great location!"
- "Good quality dogs!"
- "Tasty buns!"
- "The best English mustard!"
- "Tomato ketchup!"
- "Lashings of best quality butter!"
- "You need to do a leaflet drop in the area!"
- "Friendly staff!"
- "You need an attractive, eye-catching uniform!"

Halbert let them continue shouting for a few minutes and then finally stopped them and said, "No, what you really need to have for a successful hot dog stand is a starving crowd."

All of the things the audience mentioned were valid, but all were useless without a hungry crowd. Who is *your* starving crowd?

Find your starving crowd (otherwise known as a "niche")

If you know your customer and you know the market you compete in. then you are armed with the knowledge to combine that information so you can find small niche pockets within the larger generic market.

Every market has gaps that present opportunities for the smart and nimble small business. Large organizations can't move quickly. They have rigid systems and delivery methods, and can't cater for all needs within that market. Their one-size-fits-all-approach often doesn't meet the needs of customers that want something a little different. Think of your market as being like Swiss cheese, and find the gaps that no one else is filling.

Often we will look at our own business and say to ourselves – "Yeah, but I'm just a plumber; I don't have a niche market." And that may certainly be true. If you're a plumber, you can fix anyone's drains – regardless of where they live or what they do for a living – but you can still choose a target group.

Say you compete with ten other plumbers in your area. There is nothing much that separates you in the eyes of the consumer – you each have your own van with the common slogan, "No job too small". You each have the same experience and qualifications and you each advertise in the local business directory. So you investigate your current customer base. You are reminded of a couple of customers who wanted you to come and fix a problem before or after work because both parents were working. There is an opportunity there… If this was a problem for two of your clients, isn't it possible that it's a problem for other people? By highlighting these possibilities you can tailor your message to appeal to working professionals in need of after-hours plumbing services. Identifying and meeting that market niche doesn't of course prohibit you from working with other people in the market – it just means your message will cut through the clutter for that particular group. And when you identify these niche groups you may be surprised to realize that customers are quite happy to pay a premium for the privilege.

Business is all about perception. If you don't have a particular niche,

38   then invent one. Say you are a dog trainer. Within reason, dog training is pretty much the same regardless of the breed. But your customers and dog owners are fanatical about their dog *and* their breed. Mrs Scott just loves her poodle and George is besotted with his chocolate brown Labrador. If both were in the market for dog training and had decided that their pampered pooch could do with some behavioural tips, then which of these courses is most likely to grab their attention:

"Dog training in the park from 2 to 3 every Sunday"

　or

"Specialist poodle training in the park from 2 to 3 every Sunday"

　or

"Specialist Labrador training in the park from 2 to 3 every Sunday"?

You are offering the same product, but you're pitching it to two segments of the market and tailoring your message accordingly. By doing that, you grab the attention of smaller niche groups rather than trying to compete in a noisy and cluttered market. You differentiate yourself.

Rookie Buster

If you don't have a particular niche, then invent one.

It can sometimes be tempting to lament the fact that people are so different. After all, if all your customers were the same, you wouldn't have to worry about target marketing and finding the niche groups; you could just have one standard message and get on with making money. Only if that were true, then chances are you wouldn't be in business at all. The only reason that small businesses survive and are not squeezed out by big business economies of scale is because people are different. And the small business is perfectly placed to adapt to those differences and prosper. You may not be able to compete with the big supermarket chain on price, but you can compete on a whole host of other factors that are becoming increasingly important to modern consumers.

Look at trends to find a competitive edge and identify your niche

What are the trends in your industry? Do you find more and more customers asking for a certain product or delivery option? Ask your sales staff or customer services team for feedback on what your customers are requesting or complaining about.

Keep in mind that external factors can and will change your market, so you need to be aware of:

- Technological changes and innovations in your field.
- Potential changes to legislation that may affect your industry.
- Social trends and shifts in consumer behaviour.
- Changes in fashion.

Take environmental issues, for example. Whether you believe global warming is true or just a repetition of a trend that's happened before isn't really relevant any more. What is relevant is that consumers across the board are becoming more concerned about environmental issues. Part of that is plain economics: with rising fuel costs, consumers are being forced to look at ways to cut expenses. The other issue is that a growing number of consumers genuinely want to make ethical and environmentally responsible choices. Energy efficient products and businesses are ahead of the pack in this regard and therefore if you can genuinely make environmental claims regarding your product or service, then you need to make them publicly and incorporate them into your marketing material. Draw attention to your green credentials and seek to improve them at every stage.

Coach's notes

You need to know these seven things about your individual customers:

1. Correct contact details including complete address, telephone number and email address.
2. When they first become a customer.
3. How did they become a customer? Did they respond to an advert or campaign, or was it a referral – if a referral, who referred that person?
4. How often have they bought from you and is there any pattern?
5. How much have they spent with your business since the start of your relationship? And has it increased, decreased or remained constant?
6. How much does that work out on average per year?
7. How recently did they buy from you?

Go for it! In 1947 Frank Bettger wrote a brilliant little sales book, *How I Raised Myself from Failure to Success in Selling*. In it he captures the essence of business success when he says the quickest way to get what you want is to find out what other people want and help them get it. Understanding your customers and the market you compete in allows you to do that. And doing so gives you the opportunity to see potentially lucrative gaps in the market that will make you more money *and* make your customers happier. Being able to describe your target market and customer profile is an important piece of the puzzle as you line up your sights on the bull's eye.

42 **Notes**

Notes

Your Unique Selling Proposition (USP) is the corner stone of your marketing, because it differentiates you from your competitors. This chapter will explore how to identify your USP and how to make it especially effective so that you can stand head and shoulders above your competition and win more business.

CHAPTER 3

Create a powerful USP

How to stand out from the crowd

Pick any profession, then open up your telephone directory or go online and search the local business listings and you'll be faced with pages of options. Say the lime green and blue wallpaper in the hall is visually uncomfortable and it's just got to go! You don't have the time or inclination to do it yourself, so you decide to find a local painter and pay someone else to cover it up. Where do you start? If you're lucky you might get a referral from a friend. If not you have to make a decision based on very little information. More often than not you'll pick someone at the start of the list – which is why people call themselves AAA Painter Co. But if your business is ZZZ Painter Co – how do you differentiate your business in all your advertising? The answer is – USP.

46 *What is a "USP"?*

Your Unique Selling Proposition is a positioning statement that succinctly illustrates why your business should be chosen over your competition. Despite the simplicity of the concept it's amazing just how few companies use it. Instead they try to compete in a busy market place without any differentiation and wonder why their phone doesn't ring.

Rookie Buster

Your Unique Selling Proposition is a positioning statement that succinctly illustrates why your business should be chosen over your competition.

Personally I think part of the problem is in the word "unique" – we think that our USP needs to be truly original. That we need to sell some little widget that no one in the world sells or that we need to have patented software or high-tech innovation never before experienced. Relax – it doesn't. If viewed in this context it's easy to see why so many businesses fail to recognize the need to identify their USP, and yet it could make a massive difference to their business success.

Areas to consider for USP identification

If you don't have an obvious USP then invent one! The key thing to remember is that you *must* be able to deliver on the promises you make. There is no point professing to have the biggest selection of carpets within a 50-mile radius of your store if you haven't. Customers are not stupid. In addition your USP must be specific. Bland, meaningless statements about service or quality are useless. Your USP can't be an opinion – it needs to be an objective, specific promise about your product or service.

Rookie Buster

If you don't have an obvious USP then invent one! The key thing to remember is that you *must* be able to deliver on the promises you make.

Step outside your business and look in from that perspective. Your aim is to identify the things in your business that are or could be presented as unique. What are you prepared to commit to in order to raise yourself above your competition? Your job is to make the invisible visible – what aspects of your business offer do you take for granted that perhaps your competitors don't provide?

Areas to consider for your USP:

1 Price

Using price as the way to differentiate your product or service is certainly an option, but it's fraught with danger. For a start, customers who buy purely on price can be hard work! In addition, if you position yourself as the lowest cost provider in your area and make that your USP, then you have to maintain that strategy. If your costs escalate due to

48 changes with suppliers or economic conditions, you can end up losing money. Customers may tell you it's all down to price, but in reality it very rarely is. The buying decision is complex and can be greatly swayed by numerous other factors which won't cost you anything!

2 Service

Differentiating your business through the service you deliver can be effective. The danger here is that the USP becomes generic, such as "we offer outstanding service". That is not a USP – it doesn't mean anything and is therefore not effective. Your USP must be specific, such as: "Buy a laptop from us and you will have free 24-hour technical support for 1 week to ensure you're up and running ASAP."

Remember when Burger King introduced the idea that you could have your burger your way? Up to that point both they and their major competitor McDonalds offered a fixed product. But Burger King must have watched their customers pick out the tomato or the pickle or the onion before they ate their burger, and saw this as an opportunity to differentiate themselves from their competition and set themselves apart. Not only did they gain a competitive edge, they reduced waste, which must have reduced costs, and they demonstrated their desire to give their customers exactly what they wanted, how they wanted it.

3 Delivery

People hate to wait – especially these days when everything is instant. If you sell a product, could you offer fast, efficient and guaranteed delivery as your USP? Although they don't use it any more, Domino's Pizza was transformed from a small local operation into a global brand because of one very successful USP. Domino's knew that the biggest complaint for home delivered pizza was that by the time it arrived it was either cold or it had been so long in coming that the customer wasn't hungry any more! So Domino's introduced their unique selling proposition – "Delivered to your door within 30 minutes or it's free."

4 Durability

Perhaps your product is extremely durable and will last a lifetime. If you are confident about the quality of your product, and more importantly your market appreciates that quality, then put your money where your mouth is and back that up with a lifetime guarantee as your USP: "These work boots will last longer than you do – or your money back."

A USP is just a way for a potential customer to decide on you instead of your competition. This sort of differentiation illustrates that you have extreme confidence in your product, and that is very attractive.

Obviously you have to be confident in the quality and durability of your product. You also have to be confident that your customers *want* that durability. For example, many of the Scottish cashmere companies are struggling because their market is retracting. People don't want to buy top quality craftsmanship any more. They really don't mind that their cheap imported jersey will fall apart after a few washes, because they are only going to wear it for that season anyway!

5 Exclusivity

If you only make a small quantity of your product, or you only assist a small number of people every year, then you could use that exclusivity as your USP. Remember Cialdini's *scarcity* principal from Chapter 1 – people hate to miss out. (But remember – you can't profess that only 250 were ever made if they are pouring off a Chinese production line by the million!)

Do you have a piece of machinery that no one else has? Do you have a patented process within your business that puts you ahead of the competition? Do you have an exclusive client list?

6 Convenience

Does your business offer a short cut to a solution? Does it free up time for your customer or make their life easier or simpler in some way? With the demands of modern life there is always a desire for convenience. Perhaps you are a car hire firm – by offering to drive the car to your client and complete the paperwork on their premises, you would be appealing to a certain type of customer and putting yourself ahead of the rest who do not offer such a convenient service.

How could you make it easier for your customer to buy from you?

7 Availability

People are in a hurry and they want things immediately. The video rental store Video Ezy used this to great effect when they introduced their USP – "Get it first time or get it free." They knew that people got frustrated when they came in to rent a new release and it wasn't available, so they addressed that frustration and lifted themselves above the competition in the process.

Think also about how your product or service is packaged or offered. Say for example you are an independent gardening store. Most chains only offer standard bags of products such as sand or compost, but you could allow people to buy whatever amount they need – and charge more for the privilege.

8 Warranty

Perhaps you offer an exceptionally long guarantee with your product or service, or your warranty covers more issues than your competitors. People want to feel secure in their buying decision, and guarantees and warranties can help to do that.

Hiscox Insurance has done this by drawing potential customers' attention to the fact that they pay out on more

claims than standard insurance companies do. After all, what's the
point of paying out hefty insurance premiums every month if your
claim is going to be rejected because of the small print?

9 Staff, skills and systems

Do your employees have any particular training, skill or expertise that
puts them in the forefront of their profession? Have any of your
employees won industry awards or gained any external recognition for
their skill? Customers want to know that they are getting the best
advice, and if your business is one that requires extensive qualifications and experience, then tell your customers about them. Does your
business implement efficient systems to ensure organizational excel-
lence? Is there something special about the way you conduct your
business that ensures consistent quality and delivery?

10 Product benefits

Considering the actual product or service you offer in your business,
are there any particular product benefits that are not readily known by
your customers? Often these don't have to be unique, but they may
historically be invisible to your customer.

There is a great story about the brilliant marketing strategist Claude
Hopkins, who was commissioned to help Schlitz beer in Canada in
1919. At the time Schlitz beer was suffering image problems and was
struggling. Hopkins visited the plant and was taken through the beer
making process. Although the plant was situated on the banks of Lake
Michigan, Schlitz ignored that source of water and had dug five
4,000-foot-deep artesian wells in order to obtain even purer water.
Hopkins was shown the mother yeast cell that was the result of about
2,500 different experiments to find the best possible yeast to make the
best taste. Schlitz showed him their research facility and the five different rooms made of three-foot-thick plate glass where beer was con-
densed and distilled and re-condensed for purity. And they introduced

52   him to the five different tasters who tasted the beer at five different intervals in the brewing process. They showed him the bottling plant where the bottles were cleaned and re-cleaned twelve separate times.

The company was actually not doing anything unusual – this was more or less the process all beer producers went through. But Hopkins was the first person to tell the public about this process. In so doing he made the invisible visible. He told the customer what the beer company just took for granted, and Schlitz beer went to No. 1 in the sector within six months. By telling the public about Schlitz's process, even though it was not unique, Hopkins gained a pre-emptive advantage for the company over their rivals.

So what product benefits or facts do you take for granted that your customer may find interesting or inspiring? It may be that you are already delivering above average service or your product is unique in the industry, but if you don't tell your customers about it they will never know. Make the invisible visible.

Supercharge your USP by using risk reversal

Once you've identified your unique selling proposition, you should consider adding a risk reversal to that claim. As the name suggests, this strategy simply offers a way of reversing the risk associated with making a purchase.

When two parties come together to conduct business, the buyer has to assume a certain amount of risk in that transaction – especially when dealing with a company for the first time. One of the fears we have when we are faced with a buying decision, especially a significant or important buying decision, is the fear of making the wrong choice. What happens if I buy this and it doesn't work? What happens if I change my mind? No one wants to make a mistake or look foolish, and that risk is one of the reasons people "go away and think about it" – never to return! That assumed risk is a hurdle between you and a sale.

Risk reversal simply means that you remove the risk and all the associated fears and instead offer a conclusive and reassuring reason to buy from you and not from your competitors. Say I wanted to buy a horse and after weeks of searching I'd narrowed my search down to two horses that would both be equally perfect. Which one would I buy? I would buy the one from the owner who removed all the risk for me by saying, "Take her away for two weeks and if you don't think she's the right horse for you for whatever reason I'll come and collect her." This is risk reversal, and it's extremely powerful. It lowers the hurdle so far that it's easy for your customer to step over the line.

Rookie Buster

Risk reversal simply means that you remove the risk and all the associated fears and instead offer a conclusive and reassuring reason to buy from you and not from your competitors.

The ironic aspect of risk reversal is that most businesses, if they are sensible, would in any case offer a customer a refund and an apology should something go wrong with the product or service. It's just good business – regardless of who is to blame. If you accept that in the event of you falling short of your commitment you would refund the customer's money and do whatever it takes to regain their business and trust, then why don't you just tell people that up front? If you believe in your product or service, why wouldn't you guarantee it?

Rookie Buster

If you believe in your product or service, why wouldn't you guarantee it?

54   **Important Distinction:** I'm not necessarily suggesting that you guarantee your product or service will work. For many businesses that's not possible. Say I sold hypnosis CDs – I can't really control how the customer uses the product and therefore I can't really guarantee results. But I *could* guarantee that if that customer wasn't happy they could get their money back – no questions asked. All I'm trying to do is to remove the fear that someone has about making a wrong choice and wasting money. I may be extremely confident that my hypnotic CDs will work if the customer uses them regularly, but my confidence needs to be transferred to the customer. And besides, at the end of the day I also know that if they are not happy or even if they don't use the CDs, the chances of them actually returning the goods is very low. Apathy is the unsung hero of successful marketing!

Add risk reversal to your USP and you will supercharge your results. Just look at Domino's Pizza! They found out that their customers' biggest frustration was having to wait too long for their pizza. They addressed that fear through their USP and guaranteed that commit-ment through risk reversal: "Delivered to your door in 30 minutes or it's free." In doing so they revolutionized the pizza delivery business, and a global franchise was born.

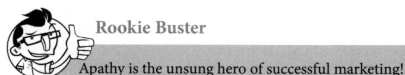

Rookie Buster

Apathy is the unsung hero of successful marketing!

You will realize by now that defining your USP and adding an addi-tional punch to that statement through a strong guarantee is not for the fainthearted – it requires that you believe in your business 100 per cent.

The easiest way to use the idea of risk reversal to maximum effect is to tap into your customers' greatest concerns and remove them. Often that is just the fear of making the wrong choice and wasting money, so a blanket money-back guarantee is powerful. Alternatively, be specific.

For example, one of the classic frustrations when dealing with builders
the world over is that a) they never arrive when they say they will, and
b) they start the job and then leave it for weeks while they finish
someone else's project.

Yet if you are a builder and you know that this is a huge frustration
for clients, and that most people have experienced this poor level of
service at some point and are therefore desperate to avoid a repeat
performance, you can tap into that fear and remove the risk – right up
front. Your USP could therefore be:

"If we are late for our appointment the repair is free!"

or

"We only build one house at a time and will be on-site every working
day until it's complete – or we'll write you a cheque for £1000!"

What scares people about using risk reversal is the fear that customers will abuse the guarantee and the business will lose money. And
yes, that is certainly a possibility – but it's very rare that it actually
happens. If someone buys something from you, and you deliver that
product or service to the absolute best of your ability, then it's unlikely
that anyone will abuse the guarantee. On the other hand, if you don't
live up to that guarantee, then you need to honour it and use the risk
reversal to demand a better and more consistent customer experience
in the future.

Risk reversal as a quality control for your business

Adding a risk reversal element to your
offer has the added advantage of raising
your business to a higher consistent standard of operation. What you will find is the
creation of a virtuous circle. By drawing
your customers' attention to your unique
selling proposition you differentiate
yourself from the competition. By guar-
anteeing the delivery of that USP you

56 remove any and all risk of that person regretting the buying decision. That will in turn raise your business game because you don't want to have to give anyone their money back. Your customer service and delivery improves, and your customer is thrilled. And happy customers are much more likely to keep buying and refer you to other people.

A USP with strong risk reversal gets your foot in the door, and in a highly competitive marketplace that's essential.

Coach's notes

Identifying a USP that taps into the fears, frustrations and major concerns of your customer base and removes the risk associated with the buying decision can make your business stand out in a sea of competition.

Thinking about the industry you operate in, what are the biggest concerns and fears of your potential customer? Try and think of at least five things that worry your customer. If you're not sure, ask your sales team for feedback about the objections they hear when trying to make a sale. What holds customers back from making that final buying decision? It may help you to think about this question in relation to the ten headings discussed above.

1. Price (e.g.: "I'm scared I can find it cheaper…"; "Find it cheaper and we'll give you twice the difference in cash!")
2. Service (e.g.: "I need this project finished by Christmas and I'm scared it won't be…"; "We guarantee a completion date – or we pay you £1,000 every day it's overdue.")
3. Delivery.
4. Durability.
5. Exclusivity.
6. Convenience.
7. Availability.
8. Warranty.
9. Staff, skills and systems.
10. Product benefits.

Go for it! Involve your people in the process of USP identification. They may have knowledge and information about your customers that you don't have. Brainstorm some ideas and create a compelling USP that will differentiate you from your competitors. Once you've identified how you can stand out from the crowd you need to communicate it at every opportunity. Put your USP in all of your advertising, add it to your compliments slips, your letterhead, all your invoices, your website – every communication you send from the business needs to hammer home your USP. And stand by it – if you fall short, deliver on your guarantee immediately.

Notes

Once you know who your best customers are and what your USP is, then you can source powerful testimonials to back up your claims and provide third party endorsement for your business. You can tell your customers how wonderful you are, but they will only ever truly believe it if they experience it themselves – or when another customer tells them how wonderful you are!

CHAPTER 4

Create a FREE sales army through testimonials

Stand up and be counted

Testimonial marketing can make a significant difference to your ability to attract new customers, and yet it is estimated that fewer than 2 per cent of businesses use it. Obviously this form of marketing is only relevant if you have legions of happy customers, but let's face it – if you don't, then the least of your worries is how to source and use a good testimonial!

The reason why testimonials are so powerful is rooted in the psychological influencers we explored in Chapter 1. There are two factors working in tandem to make testimonials so effective – social proof and authority.

Social proof refers to how we determine what is correct by looking around us and working out what other people think is correct. We are reassured as to the correct course of action if we can see others doing the same thing. Social proof is especially effective in new situations where you are in uncharted territory. If you were to go to an expensive restaurant for the first time and were unsure which knife and fork to use for which dish, you would instinctively look around you to see

62   what others were doing. The same can be said if you were driving on a road you'd never travelled before – often you would use the behaviour of other drivers instead of road signs to determine the correct speed, and so on. This aspect of human behaviour is being discussed daily in conversations between parents and children across the globe:

Parent: "Why on earth did you roll down that muddy hill? You're filthy!"

Child: "Everyone else was doing it!"

Parent: "So if everyone else jumped off a cliff – would you?"

Rookie Buster

We are reassured as to the correct course of action if we can see others doing the same thing.

We are lemmings! And marketers and clever sales people have been using this fact against us for years. Perhaps a smart barman puts folding money into his tip jar at the start of his shift to make patrons thinks that folding money tips are normal in that establishment. This technique is allegedly used in religious revival meetings, where people are said to be primed to come forward and simulate miraculous healing so that others in the audience will think it possible and part with their hard-earned cash. This brings us neatly to the second psychological influencer – authority.

If the person who is telling us what to do or giving us advice happens to hold a position of authority, we are much more likely to be influenced by their opinion. This is part of the reason why preachers, doctors or scientists have more clout than you or I do. We put people in authority on a pedestal *without any evidence that they deserve to be there.*

The extent of this can be seen when you consider the strange world of placebo medicine. Placebos are sugar tablets or injections of distilled water which have no pharmaceutical properties and yet are shown

time and time again in medical tests to elicit the same or similar healing   63
as the real drugs. In one test a doctor administered what he thought
was the real medicine to an asthma patient who experienced a rapid
improvement. Later the doctor delivered a placebo to the same patient,
telling him that it was the same medicine, only this time the patient did
not respond. The doctor assumed that the first medicine was a real
breakthrough in asthma treatment, until he discovered that there had
been a clerical error and both treatments were in fact placebos. The
apparent explanation for the patient's different responses was that the
doctor's attitude and enthusiasm for the first treat-
ment rubbed off on the patient and he responded
as expected. He had such confidence in the
authority figure that his belief made him better!

So what has all this got to do with
marketing?

Social proof is especially potent in new
and confusing situations – which are exactly
what buying decisions can be. We are faced
with multiple options in how to spend our
money. Even if we decide to buy a new car,
we are then faced with more options about
which type of car is best. We have to decide
whether to buy or not to buy and that can cause
uncertainty. Whenever there is uncertainty we will
seek certainty. If under those circumstances we are
unconsciously influenced by what other people think and do, then we
are incredibly susceptible to their influence – whether we like it or not.
So if you can gather honest, genuine testimonials about the aspects of
your business that can worry potential customers, then you can help
alleviate that confusion and encourage them to buy. So make sure the
positive and happy experiences that your customers have with your
business are known to your market.

The key to using testimonial marketing effectively is integrity. You
can't make testimonials up! Some business people do, but customers
are not stupid, they will work it out eventually, and the bitter taste you
have left in their mouths will cost you dearly.

Rookie Buster

Make sure the positive and happy experiences that your customers have with your business are known to your market.

Testimonials – the basic principles

Be specific

Detail is important in all copywriting, and testimonials are no different. Which of the following is more powerful?
1. "Company Y provided us with great service."
2. "Company Y went the extra mile. They corrected an error we had made and drove 100 miles to make sure our print job was delivered on time."

The second one is much more powerful because it's specific. The first one is too generalized and therefore loses credibility. So rule number one is to source *specific* testimonials that draw your prospects' attention to important selling points.

Measurable

Again this relates to the level of detail in a testimonial, but specifically about *measurable* detail. Quantifying the statement in some way will add potency to the recommendation. Which is more powerful?
1. "Company X helped me to increase my revenue."
2. "Company X helped me to make an additional £20,000 within three months."

Again, the second one is more compelling, because it quantifies what Company X did for that customer. Not only is this more

believable, but it packs more punch and can really help to get a prospective client over the line.

Owned

Sometimes, depending on your business, your client may not want to "own" the testimonial – that is, to put their name to it. Say for example you are a plastic surgeon – not everyone wants their friends and family to know that they have had a boob job! So there may be times when initials or a pseudonym are appropriate – but be open about it. Otherwise have your happy clients own their testimonials. Having a testimonial from "Eileen Jeffries, Oxford" is always better than from a mysterious "E. J." There will be a suspicion that E. J. is not real. So put in the detail when you can.

That means full name and location wherever possible. Also, if you are marketing business to business, then it may also add weight to the testimonial if you provide the business type and job title.

Explain who someone is to add weight to their recommendation. If for example you sold high quality saucepans, you might have a quote about the outstanding quality of the pans and their durability from Paul Smith, London. But the power of that testimonial would be amplified if you also pointed out that Paul Smith was the head chef at the Ritz Hotel or the director of the biggest cooking school in the UK. Obviously this won't always be the case, but when the position can add weight – include it.

Get permission

This doesn't have to be a big deal, but if you ask someone for a testimonial be sure to let them know what it will be used for. Let your customer know that it may appear from time to time on marketing materials, or that you may put it on your website, for example. That way, if they have any objections they can let you know immediately.

66 *If we are influenced by third party opinion, does it matter who the third party is?*

Yes, apparently it does…

In their book *Yes! 50 secrets from the science of persuasion*, Noah J. Goldstein, Steve J. Martin and Robert B. Cialdini sought to identify, amongst other things, who we pay most attention to when it comes to seeking the correct course of action. If we are influenced by the behaviour of others and decide what is right based on what others do, was there a particular type of "other" that had more of an influence?

What's so fascinating about social proof is that if you asked someone whether or not a testimonial had any impact on their buying decision, they would swear black and blue that it didn't make a difference. And yet study after study has indicated otherwise.

To illustrate the point, the authors investigated the practice hotels have of encouraging their guests to re-use their towels. Whether customers truly believe a hotel's standard claim of environmental concern or whether they think it is nothing more than a cynical way to retain more profit doesn't seem to matter – most guests are willing to re-use their towel at least once during their stay. So the question was raised – would it be possible to improve the re-use rate just by changing the message on the cards left for guests in hotel rooms? In half the rooms, the standard card was left, urging patrons to re-use their towel for the protection of the environment. The other half of the rooms ran a message to tap into social proof. These cards just told the truth – that the vast majority of guests at the hotel re-used their towel at least once during their visit. The results showed that those guests who read the second message went on to re-use their towels *26 per cent more* than those who read the standard environmental message.

What's even more fascinating is that when the authors extended this study to relate the desired behaviour to a particular room, the response rate jumped again. So in half the rooms the standard message remained, encouraging patrons to think of the environment and re-use their towel. In the other rooms, the patrons received a message that said that most people who had previously stayed *in that particular room* had re-used their towel at least once. The result was an increase in re-use of an extraordinary 33 per cent.

Why would someone feel a greater incentive to mimic the behaviour of someone who had also inhabited the same hotel room? Social proof is the answer... Whether or not it is logical or sensible, there is an assumption that if I am in Room 101 there is a good chance that the person who was previously in Room 101 is like me. People who choose the penthouse, for example, tend to have similarities – at least economic similarities.

Social proof is the recognition that we are influenced by people like us or perceived to be like us, and this has significant implications in your quest for powerful testimonials.

If you want to persuade a particular prospect or niche audience of the validity of your product or service, then source testimonials from people who match that prospect. If your prospect is a builder, show him a testimonial from a builder or a plumber. If your prospect is a beautician, then reassure her by showing her glowing reports from other people in the beauty industry who have bought your product or service and been thrilled with the results. Ironically your product doesn't even need to be related to that industry – the reassurance comes from knowing that other people like her have bought it!

If you are marketing to a particular niche audience then use testimonials in your marketing that speak directly from and to that audience.

Testimonials can be a great way of telling customers about additional perks of your business without it looking odd! For example, when I'm helping someone to write a book we often spend a lot of time together either in person or on the phone. It's extremely important to me that I like that person and that we can both enjoy the process. I think that life is too short to work with people you don't get on with. I'm also really committed to hitting deadlines, but how do you write these things in copy? Testimonials are the answer. A client of mine wrote the following testimonial in the acknowledgement of his book, and I now use it with his blessing: "I needed a special person to help me write this book and I found that person in Karen McCreadie. I want everyone to know that Karen is a genius! Thank you, Karen, for your passion and your outstanding skill. Thank you also for working so patiently with me, meeting every deadline and making it so much fun." Maybe "genius" was excessive (just maybe!), but apart from that it was a perfect third party endorsement and it covered two key points for my business.

Rookie Buster

If you are marketing to a particular niche audience then use testimonials in your marketing that speak directly from and to that audience.

Testimonials are informal, so they can explain nuances of your offer as well as shedding light on business ethics and values. These things are often incredibly difficult to articulate in any other way without sounding pompous or halfwitted! Testimonials can sometimes offer a snapshot into the people behind the business and add a dash of personality, which like it or not is important. I also know that the testimonial above will actively *discourage* some people from contacting me. There are people in the world who don't share my views, and that's absolutely OK. I appreciate that for some people, liking who they work with doesn't matter – they are just interested in getting the job done. But I'm not one of them. I want to enjoy the process, and so this testimonial tells people that, without my having to say it. As a result, most of the people who contact me share my outlook, and I genuinely enjoy the projects I choose.

Celebrity and authority endorsements

The last type of testimonial which is also very powerful is the celebrity endorsement, or expert opinion. For some reason modern society has

elevated celebrity into an authority position of sorts. Celebrities, even 69
the C-list, *Big Brother*, 15-minutes-of-fame variety, seem inexplicably
to wield a huge amount of influence on the modern market place.

Although A-grade celebrity endorsement may not be
available to the small business person, it is worth
looking out for expert scientific opinion that can
back up your claims. If you are in a business that
already has a great deal of research and development,
then have your boffins speak about their science and
use that in your marketing. It may be that you take
their expertise for granted, but make sure you tell
your audience about their involvement – it adds weight
and credibility to your offering and can significantly
improve your marketing results.

How to develop and source testimonials

Gathering testimonials is just a matter of asking the right people and
making it part of your customer services process.

First you need to identify your best customers in terms of money
spent and length of patronage. If you have worked through Chapter 2,
then you should have this information at your fingertips. Alternatively,
simply ask your sales or customer service team who they think would
be most likely to give a testimonial about your business.

Call the customer up and have a conversation with them about
their experiences with your business. Explain that you are aiming to
develop a bank of testimonials from current clients who are happy
with the products and services your business offers.

Rookie Buster

Gathering testimonials is just a matter of asking the right people and making it part of your customer services process.

It's important that you don't put words into that person's mouth and instead allow them to talk to you freely about their experiences. You may be disappointed to find out that some customers are still with you out of habit rather than happiness, but use the opportunity to find out if there is anything you can do to improve their experience. If there is – do it!

Your job is to listen to what your best clients have to say and make notes. Ask questions that will illuminate particular aspects you want addressed, especially experiences that validate your USP. So for example if your USP is all about delivery, you need to source testimonials that talk directly about the efficiency and speed of that delivery.

Remind your client that testimonials are most powerful when they are *specific*, *measurable* and *owned*. Either ask them to send you a testimonial or (even better) suggest you write something from the notes you've made and email it to them for approval. That way you are more likely to get the testimonial and you can ensure it meets the rules above. But only paraphrase what was actually said – don't go making stuff up!

Rookie Buster

Testimonials are most powerful when they are *specific*, *measurable* and *owned*.

Make sure that the request for testimonials becomes part of the after sales service. Someone is most likely to provide a testimonial

when they have just made a purchase and are most excited about their   71
decision. People soon get used to things or forget how wonderful their
holiday was – even days after arriving home. So get in early and ask for
the testimonial.

It is also worth ensuring that your customer service staff know that
you are seeking rave reviews. That way if a customer is on the phone
and compliments the service or product, they can simply ask, "Can I
quote you on that?" All they need to do is make a note of the exact
words and get the customer's permission and it's done.

Coach's notes

Testimonials – the basic principles

1. Be specific.
2. Measurable.
3. Owned.
4. Get permission.

Go for it! Once you have some compelling testimonials from your happy clients, you need to use them in your marketing materials. That means including them in brochures or direct response marketing – being sure to use testimonials from people who are similar to the target audience of your marketing. You can also easily and cheaply add them to the homepage of your website. If appropriate leave a folder full of glowing recommendations from happy clients in your waiting area or put them on the wall in your reception. Testimonials offer powerful third party endorsement for your business, so use them and see your results soar!

Notes

Notes

Everyone knows that it's much more expensive to get a new customer than it is to keep an existing one, and yet so many businesses reserve all the really good deals for their new customers. This chapter looks at ways to reverse that trend in order to ensure you keep your customers for the long term. Seeking new customers is always wise, but be careful never to forget the ones you already have in the process.

CHAPTER 5

Increase loyalty and improve customer retention

Only the adaptable survive

The great thing about small business is that it is much more mobile. If a large chain or global brand wants to innovate, it's like turning a cruise liner around. But a small business can be flexible and truly respond to changing market conditions. The people who make the decisions are usually much closer to the customer and are therefore much more likely to be able to respond to their changing needs.

Instead of being daunted by big business, you should pity big business. Big business can't move quickly – you can. And it's quick reactions that allows a business to build relationships and customer loyalty. If your customer services staff know that they are permitted to do whatever it takes (within reason!) to ensure your customers are happy, then they can develop relationships and not just follow systems. Systems are great and can help to ensure consistent delivery, but business is fundamentally the interaction between human beings.

Rookie Buster

Instead of being daunted by big business, you should pity big business.

Why is loyalty so important?

It's just basic common sense. If you have already convinced someone to buy from you, then you have already overcome all their objections and made that sale. You've created a relationship – even if it is only a tenuous one to start with. As long as you don't mess it up, then the opportunity exists for you to develop that tentative relationship further, and eventually create raving fans and advocates of your business.

Rookie Buster

Business is fundamentally the interaction between human beings.

Fact: people do business with people they like. If they like you, they will keep doing business with you. If you help them to get what they need, they will keep doing business with you. If you mess up, but immediately say sorry and do everything you can to rectify the problem, they will keep doing business with you. The leeway you will gain just by fostering your relationships can also mean that even when you *do* make a mistake, people will forgive you far more if they like you first. If faced with a buying decision which involves someone they like plus a good product, or someone they dislike plus an excellent product – the likeable person will always win the sale.

Attrition

Your business will lose customers – it's just the nature of the beast. But *how many* you lose depends on you. You may lose some because you annoy them or because you don't deliver on your promises, and if that's the case then you deserve it. You will lose others because they stopped needing your services or stopped perceiving a need or appreciating the benefits you offered. And still others are lost to plain old-fashioned apathy.

In the right hands apathy is a powerful marketing tool, but unless you have the systems in place to counter apathy then you will lose customers who would – if asked – probably have been quite happy to buy from you.

Personal circumstances change – we put a magazine subscription on hold, or we go overseas and cancel our wine club order, fully intending to reinstate it later. But life gets in the way, or a competitor steps into the relationship, and the customer is lost.

Rookie Buster

In the right hands apathy is a powerful marketing tool.

Keeping customers happy isn't rocket science – acknowledge them, communicate with them, thank them; give them more information, better offers, more knowledge, more value, more service, better guarantees. Reward them for staying with you and make it impossible for them to leave!

Say sorry!

Your complaints policy should be very simple: if the customer who is complaining is in the 20 per cent of customers who provide 80 per cent

80 of your income, then you do whatever it takes to fix the problem and make them happy. And if they have access or influence in a network of likeminded people who could also benefit from your product or services, again do whatever it takes to keep them happy – and if you screw up, apologize in person and in style!

Make this policy known across the business so a customer never has to hear, "No, I can't help you with your complaint – the person you need to speak to is at lunch." Instead authorize your staff to handle issues on the spot. And if that's not possible, tell your staff to take all the details and promise to get back to the customer by the end of the day. And do it.

Reward customers and extend your USP

Loyalty to your business is created every time you deliver on your promises. It is also, strangely enough, fostered if you mess up and fix the problem really quickly. Loyalty is created through good offers and letting your customers see that you say what you mean and mean what you say.

All too often we see offers and special deals aimed at attracting new customers to a particular business. It's a logical approach to try and entice customers through the door, but what about your existing customers? You had better ensure that your introductory offers are not created at the expense of your existing clients. Remember, your old customers are your competitors' new customers, and if you're not careful you may find them being tempted to leave you.

Rookie Buster

Remember, your old customers are your competitors' new customers.

If you are in the business of tempting new customers, use that PR and advertising to target a special message to your existing customers at the same time. Find a way to reward them too, so they don't get annoyed if they see your advertising. Instead make the introductory offer a talking point and send them a letter saying, "You may have noticed in the local paper that we are offering a great introductory offer for new customers. Reaching new people is always important for any business, but we just want you to know we still value you too. For the duration of the introductory offer we would like to say a special thank you for being an on-going customer by offering you…"

How viable or feasible this is will depend on your business. Banking is notorious for introductory interest rates that get people through the door, and then after the initial offer period the rates quietly fade away. As a result most customers don't even realize they are on a poor deal! Offering equally good rates to all customers may not be financially viable, but even a business like a bank could find a way to reward their existing customers. Perhaps they could create a financial assessment tool or offer their existing clients a free annual review of their finances to see if there are better ways to manage their money. None of these things cost much, but they make existing customers feel appreciated, and that's extremely important if you want to keep them.

When you are looking for ways to reward your existing customers, look specifically at your USP. If they can see that your USP is true and that you live up to it, then you create trust, and trust is essential for loyalty.

Once you have established your USP, use extensions of that promise in special offers and periodic promotions. So if your USP is based on price, then make the offers a further extension of your price promise. If your USP is based on service, then offer additional service-based benefits to confirm your commitment to that.

Use special promotions to confirm to your customers that their decision to buy from you in the first place was a valid one. Make it easy for them to keep buying from you.

82 *Surprise and delight your customers*

Answer this question: "When a customer buys from me, what do they expect?" Answer the same question for your competitors and make a list of the results. Chances are your customers will expect to receive what they paid for and for it to arrive in a condition they expect within a reasonable time frame. You had better make sure that what you deliver when meeting these requirements matches what you have stated on your marketing and sales material.

But you should be interested in delivering *more* than expected. Perhaps you notice that everyone in the industry delivers within seven days. Is it possible to turn your orders around in 48 hours? Once you've delivered on your core promises, find ways to make the delivery process extraordinary. Add extra units as a thank you for the third order this month, offer additional discounts or add a bag of jelly babies to the order to sweeten their day! Whatever you do make it random and make sure you tell them why you've done it – draw their attention to the added extra otherwise they a) might not notice it, or worse, b) assume it's just part of the service. If you do something every time, people become complacent and the added value is lost. Plus when you stop doing it the customer feels cheated!

Listen to your customers

What are your customers telling you? Ask your customer services team or your dispatch personnel if they hear recurring themes. Is there something your customers want that you are not supplying? Apart from offering you valuable insight from the sharp end into how your business is running and how it could be improved, showing that you are listening to your customers inspires loyalty. Everyone wants to be heard, so where appropriate use that feedback to improve your service.

Find out what your customers' end goal is and help them achieve it. Remember Bettger's advice from Chapter 2 – the quickest way to get what *you* want is to find out what *other people* want, and help them get it. If you can do that, you don't just gain a customer – you gain an advocate for life.

Rookie Buster

Find out what your customers' end goal is and help them achieve it.

I wrote a book for a client in Australia in early 2008. This client had already written a book himself, but didn't have the time to write the next one, so he contacted me to see if I would write it for him. I did, and he was really happy with the manuscript, but when his original publisher took too long to produce the finished book, he decided to self-publish. He had a natural market as an international speaker, so was confident he could recoup the costs quickly. He contacted me to see if I knew anyone else who could help him. I knew his end goal was to get the book produced fast, so I gave him the contact details for an editor, a proofreader and a designer I had used in the past. I gained nothing from giving him that information, especially as book writing isn't exactly a repeat sale sort of product, but I wanted to make sure he achieved his goal. He was thrilled! I helped him get what he wanted when he wanted it, and as a result he is a passionate advocate of my work. Within just a couple of months of completion, he had already referred me to several other people in his network.

Go out of your way to help your clients – even if there is no benefit or obvious advantage for you to do so.

84 *Stay in touch*

If apathy is the primary cause of excessive attrition rates, then one of the best ways to avoid apathy is to stay in the minds of your customers. Keeping in consistent contact will mean that they are far more likely to think of you when the time comes around to buy what you sell.

If you stay out of sight for too long, you will stay out of mind. So you need to find meaningful and useful ways to stay in touch with your customers. There was a time when a printed newsletter was a good idea, and if you happen to be a printer it possibly still is, but for the rest of us it's rarely a good use of money.

Online newsletters or e-zines make keeping in touch much more feasible for the small business. So gather email addresses and be sure to get your customers' permission to contact them a few times a year to inform them of the latest offers. If you decide on an e-zine, make sure that 80 per cent of the content is customer focused and that it's chock full of helpful tips or useful information. Remember – it's not about you: it's about finding ways to help your customers to reach their goals. Perhaps you could let them know of legislative changes that might affect them, or perhaps there is a way you can educate your customer so they get more from your product or service.

Rookie Buster

Remember – it's not about you: it's about finding ways to help your customers to reach their goals.

Up-sell and cross-sell

People are often reluctant to communicate with their customers because they don't want to be a pest. Certainly receiving generic mailers containing the latest offers or newest promotion without any regard for what the customer has previously purchased can be irritating.

But if that communication is targeted and personalized, then it can be a win–win situation.

Say for example I buy cosmetics products from you. You know from my buying history that I have a penchant for a particular brand – you can safely assume that I would be interested in a sale of that brand. I would be even more likely to respond if you personalized the message and offered a special discount for my loyalty. If I only had a short time to respond and I knew the offer was limited to a few specially selected customers I'd be still more likely to respond.

If I only ever buy a certain product, I might be tempted to try additional products in the range. This is known as "cross-selling". Look at other products or services that you already supply and how your customers might benefit from them too.

If you know your customer and what they need and want, then you also have the opportunity to upgrade their purchase to a better product. This is known as "up-selling" and it's used in the electronics industry a great deal. By advertising the lowest prices, retailers get people in the door so they can then interview the customer and where appropriate direct them to a product with a higher specification that is more suited to their needs.

I had to buy a new laptop recently. I'd been putting it off for months because I was overwhelmed by the choice and didn't really understand what I needed. In the end I went with an online company that tempted me in with good price deals, and more importantly they offered telephone support so that you could tell someone what you needed and they would recommend a product. After briefly explaining what I wanted the machine to do, I followed the advice I received and plumped for a fairly basic machine. All I do on the laptop is write, so I didn't need a massive memory or fancy graphics packages, but now I wish I'd been up-sold! With hindsight I wish I had spent an extra £150 and got a really good machine. Initially I was encouraged that I wasn't being sold something fancy I had no use for, but there is a happy medium. It was in my best interests to sell me something that I was going to be thrilled with. I wasn't up-sold to a better product and as a result I was unhappy and the business missed out on additional income. It ended up being not a win–win but a lose–lose. You have to genuinely match your client's needs with your best solution.

Remember, getting people in the door for the first time is the hardest part. Once they have bought from you they are much more responsive to your message because they have a history with you, even if it's a short one.

Offering your clients alternatives and choices is just good business. It shows you are listening to their needs; recognize their buying history and you build loyalty to your business. Up-selling and cross-selling are important because they benefit your customers. And that ultimately benefits your bottom line.

Rookie Buster

Offering your clients alternatives and choices is just good business.

Increase all your staff's sales skills

People panic at this, but it's really just a simple and subtle shift in the conversation. I was in the supermarket on the afternoon I was writing this chapter and I bought a chocolate bar. At the checkout the cashier said to me, "This one is 51p but if you bought the pack of five on special, it's only £1." Granted that this is not high finance, and certainly I didn't need five chocolate bars, but I bought them! I was glad to be told of the offer because I felt as though the cashier knew her business and was looking out for me. I spent more money in the shop and it strengthened my loyalty to that small supermarket chain.

This is what I mean about increasing the sales skills – it's just about having your employees know what offers and possibilities exist in your company so that they can help the customer get the best product or price they can.

There is a large UK chain store (which shall remain nameless) which has clearly got this wrong. Whatever you buy they are obviously told always to ask customers, "Would you like some stamps or a mobile

phone top-up with that?" Why on earth would I want stamps when
I've just bought deodorant and two packs of tissues? It's not a natural
part of the conversation and just comes across as forced and stilted.
Plus it's really annoying!

Coach's notes

Seven steps to loyal customers

1. Say sorry!
2. Reward them and extend your USP.
3. Surprise and delight your customers.
4. Listen to them.
5. Stay in touch.
6. Up-sell and cross-sell.
7. Increase the sales skills of all your staff.

Go for it! Good marketing on a budget comes from being smart about the resources you already have, and learning how to maximize those resources. Your current customers are a massive resource for you. These are people you have already sold to; you've already countered their objections and provided them with a quality product or service. Your job is to keep them happy over the long term; the initial sale is the start of the relationship, not the end of it. Keep in touch and add genuine value. It's much cheaper and smarter to make sure the customers you have stay loyal than to waste buckets of cash on the constant pursuit of new ones.

90 **Notes**

Notes

You don't have to be a marketing guru to know that the best advertising is "word of mouth". If faced with a buying decision, there is nothing more compelling than a referral from someone we know, like or trust. Birds of a feather flock together, so we can safely assume that your customers know other people who could benefit from your services. This chapter looks at how to access this lucrative resource.

CHAPTER 6

Ask for referrals

Work with people you like

In Chapter 2 we discussed the importance of data and crunching a few numbers in relation to your current customer base. One of the reasons for that was so you could establish whether your best (and worst) customers share any similarities. This customer profile allows you to source ways to access other people who share those similarities, or to avoid marketing to people who share the similarities highlighted by your worst customers. Business isn't just about making money – you should enjoy the process and get a sense of satisfaction from working. If you can identify the thorns in your business side, then do so. Choose to work with people you like and who appreciate you, and leave the rest for someone else.

Rookie Buster

Business isn't just about making money – you should enjoy the process and get a sense of satisfaction from working.

If you are able to differentiate the various customers in your business, then you can seek more of the ones you want and fewer of the ones you don't want. If you find that your best clients share a number of characteristics, then it's highly likely that they will know people in their social or business network who also share those characteristics.

Just think of your own network of friends for a moment. Is it true to say that you have pockets of likeminded people in that larger group? For example, you may have friends from art class or from the gym, and you may have friends from work and friends from school, but the idea of putting your art class group with your kickboxing buddies brings you out in a cold sweat. Yet you get on with all of them because of different aspects of your nature. The same is true in business circles.

What is a referral?

Quite simply a referral is asking your existing happy customers if they know anyone else who might be interested in also benefiting from your product or service.

Often businesses feel it would be an imposition to ask their customers for referrals – after all, if they are happy they will tell people anyway – right? Actually, no, they usually won't! One of the mysteries of human behaviour is that an unhappy client will tell everyone within a 50-mile radius just how rubbish you've been, yet a happy client will rarely mention it unless specifically asked. This is why it's so important to fix problems and fix them fast. In many ways it doesn't matter whose fault it is – just fix it, because an unhappy customer can do a great deal of damage to your business.

If you want referrals, you have to specifically ask for them. And you need to change the way you view this process. Instead of thinking of it as an imposition, look at it as an opportunity for your clients to feel warm and fuzzy about doing a helpful thing for their friends and associates. We've all experienced the pleasure of recommending someone and having the person come back and thank us later. I often recommend editors, designers or proofreaders in the course of my work, and it's a wonderful feeling to have both parties come back and thank me for the introduction. It's a win–win for everyone.

Rookie Buster

If you want referrals, you have to specifically ask for them.

If you are passionate about your business and are committed to delivering the best possible service, then why wouldn't you want as many people as possible to experience it? You owe it to your customers – especially your really loyal, happy customers – to give them the opportunity to share their experiences and help those they care about.

So why don't we ask for referrals?

It's a simple idea and at face value it makes sense to everyone. We refer people to things all the time in normal, everyday life. Say for example you took your partner to the new Italian restaurant that opened nearby and you were blown away by their homemade tiramisu. Or perhaps you finally decided to join the local gym and couldn't get over how helpful and knowledgeable the fitness instructors were. Or maybe you discovered a little boutique clothes shop that imports beautiful hand-stitched silk garments from around the world.

And you'd tell people. More often than not it will come up in conversation and you'll be reminded to say how great the Italian restaurant was, or perhaps a friend will ask you if you have any recommendations, and that restaurant will immediately spring to mind.

Regardless of how it comes about, you are more than happy to share

96   your experiences and have no qualms about recommending their services. Yet why don't the same rules apply in business?

The answer is reciprocity.

Remember in Chapter 1 we talked about the six basic principles of psychology that direct human behaviour, as identified by Robert B. Cialdini. One of those was reciprocity – the innate need for fairness and balance in a relationship.

The reason most businesses don't implement a referral system is because traditionally the referral request is tacked on to the end of a sales process. Or someone – usually the sales person who made the sale or someone in customer services – is charged with calling the client a few days after they have received their goods to ask for a referral. The idea is that when someone has just bought they are hopefully most happy with the purchase and are more likely to respond.

But the problem with this approach is that the equation is balanced at that point. The customer has paid the money and the goods have been dispatched. There is symmetry and balance in that relationship. If someone then asks for a referral, that delicate balance is disrupted and the business is seeking the effect of reciprocity, not causing reciprocity to occur. The business is asking for a favour and it feels odd to the person asking for the referral so they just don't so it.

That's why referral systems don't work. Because people don't ask! And they don't ask because it feels weird. And it feels weird because the person asking for the referral has put themselves at the mercy of reciprocity. They feel as though they have asked for something for no reward or reciprocal benefit to the other person – like asking a favour.

There are two ways to counter this:

1. Honest flattery.
2. Incentivize the referral.

Honest flattery

Say you have a great client, they are so easy to work with, they live locally and they always pay on time. They make regular orders and you have a really good relationship with that person. As a result you are pretty keen to find more people like him.

The first option is that you just tell him that! Be honest. Call your client and say, "I'm just calling because I'm looking for another you! Now that may not be entirely possible but even someone similar would be great. I'm looking for another customer that is …" You fill in the blank here – just be genuine and explain the characteristic that you most admire about working with that client. And finish by asking: "So come on, who do you know that's like that?"

Be sure to ask open questions such as "Who do you know…?" rather than closed questions like "Do you know…?" You want people to engage in the question rather than just find easy ways to close down the conversation.

Rookie Buster

You want people to engage in the question rather than just find easy ways to close down the conversation.

In business we very rarely take time to acknowledge someone else, especially clients. This approach is a win–win because it's genuine and it reminds your client how enjoyable your working relationship is and how much benefit he gets from that relationship. It also gives them a little buzz to know you have acknowledged them. Everyone enjoys genuine praise and recognition. Everyone! Even if that client doesn't give you any names – he is going to feel good about the call and that can only strengthen his loyalty to your business. And when he does think of someone, he just might call you up!

Obviously this won't work if you use generic, bland statements, so where possible back up what you say with evidence – remind the customer of a situation or experience you've shared that illustrates your point.

By approaching your best customers in this way you remove that feeling of unease, because you are giving your customers something

98   really valuable and enjoyable – genuine recognition. You are also giving them an opportunity to strengthen their own network by introducing a valuable product and service to other people. Plus it doesn't cost much!

Incentivize the referral

The other way to remove that feeling of imbalance caused by reciprocity is to incentivize the referral. This means that there is a tangible benefit for the customer in exchange for the referral.

There are two ways to do this. The first is to offer the customer an incentive that directly benefits him or her. That may include additional discounts on future orders or extensions to service. For example, if you were a tax accountant and you wanted to increase your customer base, you might approach your best customers and suggest that if they refer two people whom they feel could also benefit from your tax advice, then they will receive a 50 per cent reduction in the cost of next year's tax service. You could run this as a standard annual strategy, giving your best clients the opportunity to halve their tax preparation bill each year while gradually increasing your client base.

If you owned a health club you could use referral to increase your membership. Most people prefer to go to the gym with a friend anyway, so you could offer extended access to club facilities for the member and their friend for three months. Not only does it not cost you anything to offer this, but it may lead to an upgrade in the membership for both your original member and the friend. Ideally, find ways to add value that don't necessarily cost you money. For example, five free passes to the steam room would be better than a gym bag, because the steam room is already on all the time anyway and you'd have to purchase the gym bags.

The other way to incentive the referral is to

offer a discount to the customer's contact. This approach is particularly effective because it allows your client to "balance the books" with his contact. Say you called your good client Susan Williams and told her that you were looking for more clients like her. What people often fail to appreciate is that if you ask Susan for some names of people you could contact and she tells you to call Ian Scott she will automatically feel an obligation and responsibility to Ian. The imbalance has occurred in that relationship now as well. This imbalance can be removed by incentivizing the referral so that Ian receives a genuine advantage from the contact.

Rookie Buster

Ideally, find ways to add value that don't necessarily cost you money.

Going back to the tax accountant example, Susan is really happy with the service you offer. You are constantly alerting her to new tax legislation that might affect her and as a result you have legitimately saved Susan thousands in her annual tax bill. Chances are she'd be more than happy to refer you to Ian. If by referring Ian and Molly she gets a discount of 50 per cent on next year's bill, and both Ian and Molly receive a thorough assessment and 10 per cent off their initial bill, then everyone wins.

Yes, you may lose a little income, but it's much cheaper than creating a marketing campaign or advertising in the local paper. Plus Ian and Molly are Susan's friends, so they are likely to end up being really great customers too. And once you've proved yourself to them, you can offer the same referral benefits to them as well, confident in the knowledge that they too will happily generate leads for you.

If you offer benefits to everyone in the chain, then no one feels awkward and everyone wins. A word of warning, however – you had better make quite sure that you deliver on your commitment to your

100 customers' referral contacts. Otherwise you risk losing not only the referral but your valued customer too. When your customer passes on contact details of people they know and like, then they are by default assuming some responsibility for that transaction. If you let that client's friend down, you let the client down too, and they will probably never forgive you for it. You've made that client look stupid because their judgement about you was obviously flawed. So if you are going to instigate a referral system into your business you must be absolutely sure you can efficiently cope with demand and deliver impeccable service and quality in order to make your client look like a hero, not an idiot.

Rookie Buster

If you offer benefits to everyone in the chain, then no one feels awkward and everyone wins.

Got the name – now what?

When you're asking for referrals it's important to a) find out as much as possible about that person from your customer, and b) get your customer to call ahead and tell their contact that you will be calling.

This is why asking for referrals is better done face-to-face or in a phone conversation, because you can ask the contact about the person involved as part of the conversation. It doesn't need to be a big deal. Ask your customer why that person's name came to mind. If you offer a range of products or services, ask your customer which part of your range they think would be of most interest to that person and why. Ask what they like and respect about that person and why they think you may be able to help them.

Rookie Buster

Asking for referrals is better done face-to-face or in a phone conversation.

And most importantly of all, ask them to call and introduce you so that when you do follow up, they are expecting to hear from you.

How you choose to follow up will depend on the product or service. For example, a higher margin product or service would do better with a telephone follow-up, whereas that may not be cost effective for a smaller margin product. In which case you may wish to instigate a referral campaign and send your contacts an invitation to provide one or two referrals. Be sure to follow the same rules as every other form of marketing and make a compelling offer. If you have the resources you may then follow up the mailing campaign with a telephone call to increase response.

Side benefits

Instituting a referral system in your business will also assist in creating a customer focused culture. If your customer services representatives and sales people know that there is going to come a point in the buying cycle where they are going to have to ask that customer for referrals, then it is going to focus their attention on providing the best possible service, and building the strongest possible relationship. And that can only be good for the customer and the business.

A referral process also assists in customer loyalty, because of the psychological driver of consistency. Consistency is the drive to remain true to our initial choices; we want to be or appear to be consistent. If I'm your customer, then I've already made the choice to buy from you; if I go one step further and recommend your business to a friend of mine, then I am even more committed to your business. That

102   additional action confirms my initial choice and makes me even more loyal to the business.

Rookie Buster

A referral process also assists in customer loyalty, because of the psychological driver of consistency.

Remember, consistency is also working against you when you are trying to win a new customer away from your competition. Apathy is a powerful force in its own right, but add a dash of consistency and it can be hard to prise a customer away from your competition. Your competitors have to be either really bad or you have to be really good. As you have no control over how well your competition performs, focus on making your own business really *really* good!

Coach's notes

Simple rules to follow for referral systems

1. Identify your best customers and look at them as dear and valued friends. Treat them with the same care and concern you would your other friends.
2. Acknowledge the value and benefit you bring to your customers (if you can't do that you're in a whole lot of trouble).
3. Hold yourself and your business to the highest standard on behalf of your customers' best interests.
4. Gather together a group of three or four key people from sales, customer service and dispatch, and brainstorm some ideas of how you could create a referral system and what you could use to incentivize it.
5. Choose the best idea, cost it so you don't have any nasty surprises further down the road, and then test it.
6. Find a referral offer that is compelling and implement it across the business.
7. Brainstorm ways to reward all your staff for using the referral system and for bringing new clients into the business.

Go for it! Marketing is about being smart about who you need to talk to and finding the quickest and easiest way possible to open up that conversation. If you already have a list of happy clients who are buying from you on a regular basis, then it's safe to assume they know other people who would or could also benefit from your services. So ask them and make it worth everyone's while. That includes the person asking for the referral, the person being asked for the referral, and the referral themselves. Win–Win–Win!

Notes

The words you use to describe your product or service are extremely important. Good writing is not a mysterious dark art; there are hall-marks to powerful copy writing and that makes it possible to learn. This chapter will explore some of those essential elements so you can learn to improve your message and gain more confidence in your writing.

CHAPTER 7

How to write copy that sells

What are you writing?

First things first – what are you writing? Every communication that comes from your company is a marketing opportunity, so what you say in everything from an email to a glossy corporate brochure matters!

Chances are, however, if you are reading this chapter, that you want to write some sort of marketing material. Perhaps you need a brochure for your sales team to leave behind with prospective customers, or you want to create an inexpensive flyer that can be dropped in neighbourhood letterboxes, or maybe you want to create an eye-catching poster or an advert for the local paper.

Don't waste your time and money producing something without a really good reason. Think about what it is you want to write. Why do you want it? Did it just sound like a good idea at the board meeting, or has someone done some research into this? Consider how the item will be used – will it be posted? If so, make sure you comply with postal regulations on shape and size, or the cost of postage could be a nasty surprise come delivery time. Who is going to use this item? And ultimately what do you want it to do? If the answer is anything other than "sell more product", then is it really necessary? Educating your customers and building your brand are only relevant to a small business when coupled with a strong sell.

> ### Rookie Buster
>
> Educating your customers and building your brand are only relevant to a small business when coupled with a strong sell.

Regardless of whether you're writing a corporate brochure, a direct marketing letter, a flyer, poster or postcard, all sales and marketing copy has five crucial ingredients that come together to make good writing:

1. Voice.
2. Central premise.
3. Structure.
4. Style.
5. Detail.

Voice

When you create a marketing message, whether that is through a sales letter or web copy, you are creating a "personality" from which that message is coming. That is the voice of your marketing and you need to ensure that it matches your business. For example, if your business is known for its safety record and conjures images of security and reliability, delivering a flippant, almost humorous marketing message would confuse your audience and damage your brand. One way to think about this is to ask the question, "If this product or service was a person, how would they talk to the prospective customer?"

The voice of your marketing is not always obvious and you can't

point to it. Often, like good structure, you don't even notice it until it's   109
wrong! It's the essence of what the writing conveys in terms of the feelings it creates in the reader. As a good starting point it is helpful to have
a friendly voice when writing marketing copy – a conversation between
two old friends is usually beneficial to a sale. Many companies have
however used a different voice to great effect; think of Nike – "Just do
it!" The voice in that instance is more demanding, like an irritated drill
sergeant reminding us of the things we know we need to do.

If you get clear on the voice of the message and what feelings and
emotions that voice should generate in the audience, then you are
already in a far stronger position to ensure you get the actual writing
right.

Rookie Buster

When you create a marketing message, you are creating
a "personality" from which that message is coming.

Often this information will naturally flow from the overall strategy
of the business, and all the preceding chapters about target audience
and market segmentation will also help you to match the right voice to
the right audience.

Central premise

Good marketing copy should be the fleshing out of one central premise
or big idea. So say for example you make tradesmen's tools and you've
decided that your USP is durability. Everything from the graphics you
use (perhaps an elephant sitting on the workbench) to the headline to
the message and offer should be around the central premise of durability. If you start mixing your message, the reader gets confused, and
confused readers don't buy.

110 Keep the message simple and straightforward, and don't muddy the waters with too many ideas.

Structure

As Lewis Carroll wrote in *Alice's Adventures in Wonderland*, "Begin at the beginning, and go on till you come to the end: then stop."

Good writing – of any kind – has a beginning, a middle and an end. The beginning should reiterate but not repeat the headline you've chosen. After all, the reason they even got to the beginning is because the headline caught their attention, so expand on what they are obviously interested in. The middle is where you build your case and put all your selling facts and details. But stay focused on the central premise. And finally the end is the call to action, telling the reader what they should do right now to buy the product. Include all the details to convert into a sale. In sales letters use PS messages to reiterate your offer – people always read them.

Style

The golden rules are:
1. Edit ruthlessly; make every word count.
2. Use nouns and verbs and avoid too many adjectives and adverbs.
3. Use simple sentence structure and keep sentences short.
4. Say what you mean and mean what you say.
5. Don't use a long word when a small one will do.

Detail

Good writing is specific and concrete and bad writing uses abstract generalities that are weak and unimpressive.

Detail brings copy to life and adds weight and certainty to the offer. Marks & Spencer's food advertising has used this technique brilliantly. M&S don't advertise apple pie and custard – they advertise "British Bramley apple pie smothered in creamy Channel Island custard". M&S don't advertise beef burgers – they advertise "Herb crusted British beef melt in the middle burgers filled with creamy Italian Gorgonzola cheese." M&S don't advertise roast lamb – they advertise, "Farm assured British lamb topped with red onion and rosemary with a fruity port and damson sauce." The detail induces imagery in the mind that makes the words come alive and as a result you almost start salivating. And that's exactly what they want.

Rookie Buster

Detail brings copy to life and adds weight and certainty to the offer.

Remember the story of Claude Hopkins and Schlitz beer – the reason his copy was so powerful was because he went to the bother of finding out the details in the product development stage and then drew the customer's attention to those details. It didn't matter that all other beers did the same thing; what mattered was that the customer did not previously know about it. The explanation of that detail took the company to the No. 1 position in just six months.

Be very precise in your choice of words. Talk about "wool" instead of "material". Talk about "Maris Piper potatoes" instead of "vegetables". Don't talk about craftsmanship if you can instead demonstrate that craftsmanship by describing the processes involved. That way the

112 reader doesn't need superlatives – they draw their own conclusion about the level of skill involved.

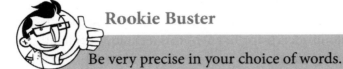

Rookie Buster

Be very precise in your choice of words.

The detail should however only flesh out that central premise. It must be relevant to the message you are delivering, so that it validates your proposition and differentiates you from your competitors.

Also remember the essence of the words you use. There are over a million words in the English language. That's a lot of possible words. Most people regularly use just a few thousand. It's important that you use words people understand, but try and be as precise as possible and craft a mental image with the words you choose. Use words that allow people to paint a very clear and precise picture in their head of what you're offering and the benefits your product will bring to their life.

The imagery that is created by good writing is important in getting your customers to take action. If through your words you can paint a picture that inspires the customer, then you've succeeded. A great way to create powerful imagery in your writing is through the use of metaphor. Porsche 911 Turbo used this brilliantly when they compared their car to a thoroughbred racehorse and expanded the copy along those lines. Metaphor gives the reader a deeper appreciation for what you are trying to say and expresses things that words alone can't. It's particularly useful when you have to get your point across in just a few words.

Always talk about benefits, not features

I was reminded of just how important this is recently when I was in the market for that new laptop I mentioned in Chapter 5. As I searched online I was faced with page after page of technical information that might as well have been written in Greek for all the sense it made.

"Intel Celeron M530 – 1.73GHz, 533 MHz FSB 1MB L2 cache, 1GB RAM, 80GB 5400rpm, DVD-Super Multi double-layer drive, 14.1" WXGA CrystalBrite TFT LCD 1280 x 800 ExpressCard/54, 3xUSB, VGA, S-Video, Wireless 802.11b/g, built-in microphone and stereo speakers, 44.4W 6-Cell Li-ion battery, 2.6kg..."

I was thoroughly confused! What is the difference between a Pentium and a Celeron processor? Considering what I needed the laptop for, would I even be able to tell the difference? What size of processor did I need and what on earth did dual core or quad core actually mean?

I knew what I needed it to do, but no one talked to me in that language. I knew the benefits I was after, but everyone was talking features. Your customer will not automatically make the mental leap between the features your product or service offers and the benefits they will translate into – *you* need to make that leap for them.

Talk about the customer, not yourself

The biggest mistake you can make in your marketing copy is to talk about yourself. The reader doesn't care! The reader doesn't care whether you've been in business for thirty years unless and until you can tie that experience back to how you are going to solve your potential client's problems. The reader doesn't care what new machinery you've invested in or new staff you've recruited or even what patents you own – unless those things are going to solve their problem. They want to know if your product or service can make them happier, sexier, healthier, richer or safer. They want to know what you can do for them, *not* what they can do for you.

Rookie Buster

The biggest mistake you can make in your marketing copy is to talk about yourself.

We are being continually bombarded by advertising messages from the TV, newspapers, radio and internet or just when walking down the street. As a result we are getting very good at ignoring a great deal of them. You know this yourself – when are you most likely to pay attention to information about car insurance? When your car insurance is due for renewal. Any other time you see advertising about it – you hit the mute button on your TV or file the mailer in the bin. Have you ever had the experience of deciding to buy a new car and then suddenly seeing that car everywhere or noticing the advertising for it? It's not that a surge of that particular car arrived on the planet, it was just that the new car came on to your internal radar and you started to notice it. The same is true of advertising.

Your job is to find out what your customers want and present yourself as the solution. The fact that you have patents pending or 50 years' experience is then important to *validate* their decision to buy from you. But it is never the *reason* – the decision itself was made because you demonstrated to the customer that you understood their "unique" challenge and were able to solve it.

Rookie Buster

Your job is to find out what your customers want and present yourself as the solution.

Make a compelling offer   115

Your marketing copy should address your target market, and if you've done a good job you will have articulated the challenge they face and aggravated that problem so they are motivated to find a solution. All you have to do now is make an irresistible offer! You need to provide a compelling argument as to why someone should take action *right now*. The main ways to do this are through a combination of price, incentives and scarcity.

Price

If you are using price as the bargaining chip, then you need to demonstrate a significant saving if the customer buys now.

Incentives

Offers that include an extra "free gift" or bonus offer are often very effective. These items are especially powerful if they have a high perceived value and/or they are directly linked to the initial product or service. For example, wine clubs often offer expensive bottle openers or cooking knives if the customer orders before a certain date.

Scarcity

Good marketing copy should not be open ended. You need to target your campaign and give it an end date. Remember Cialdini in the opening chapter – one of the biggest psychological drivers we have is the desire not to miss out on something. This is why effective marketing campaigns have a closing date or a limited number on offer. That innate desire not to miss the opportunity, coupled with price discounts and incentives to act now create a compelling offer.

116 *Warning!*

Before you offer up bonus incentives and slashed prices – cost it! Make sure you cost it based on both worst-case and best-case scenarios. Do you have the internal capacity and operational efficiency to cope with a surge of orders, or are you just going to annoy your customers? Do you have enough of the bonus items to satisfy potential demand?

If you're unsure just how important this is, cast your mind back some years to what is commonly known as the "Hoover Fiasco". Hoover offered two free return flights to Europe when you spent £100 or more on Hoover products. In an era before cheap air travel this was a really attractive offer and the response was massive. Hoover were so excited by the initial enthusiasm that they extended the offer to include flights to the USA. It was corporate suicide. They were woefully unprepared both for the response and for the financial and administrative implications. Disgruntled customers eventually took the company to court in a case that dragged on for four years, and the campaign ended up costing Hoover £50 million. It is to this day widely cited as one of the biggest corporate mistakes of all time.

Write in the first and second person

Good writing, especially good marketing copy, should sound like a conversation between two people who like each other! The writing should sound like it's coming from a real person who is 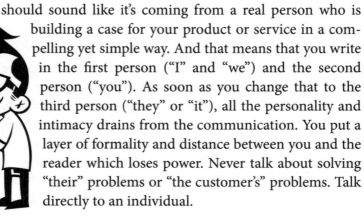 building a case for your product or service in a compelling yet simple way. And that means that you write in the first person ("I" and "we") and the second person ("you"). As soon as you change that to the third person ("they" or "it"), all the personality and intimacy drains from the communication. You put a layer of formality and distance between you and the reader which loses power. Never talk about solving "their" problems or "the customer's" problems. Talk directly to an individual.

Consider which is more powerful:

"We have found that people with sore backs find that our product solves their problem."

"You don't have to suffer any more. Our product is proven to ease lumbar pain."

Now, assuming you've got your targeting right, the second version is far more active and personal. The other problem with third person language is that it is easy to then slip into the passive voice. The passive voice avoids responsibility and is not effective, especially not in marketing.

There are those in corporate positions who would swear blind that business to business marketing is different to consumer marketing. Certainly there are nuances you need to consider, but the fact remains that businesses don't make buying decisions – people do. You have to talk to a person, not an entity.

Rookie Buster

Businesses don't make buying decisions – people do.

Action points to improve your writing

Take a piece of writing you've done recently, and read it again. Read it out loud.

1. Does it sound conversational? If not, change it until it does. For example, use contractions; instead of writing "I could not", change it to "I couldn't".

2. Do you run out of breath when you're reading the sentences? If so, break them up. Put the main point up front and then add the additional detail as separate sentences that follow.

3. Is there any jargon or technical language? If so, either remove them or fully explain them in lay terms. But don't use them unless it's absolutely necessary. Do you have to re-read sections to understand them? If so, re-work them to simplify the message – no one likes a smart-arse!

4. Are you using the active voice? Do you write about "they" or "you"? Always write to a person, it's more conversational and friendly.

5. Are there any extra words or phrases that are unnecessary? Get rid of superlatives and unnecessary adjectives.

6. Where is the focus? You need to be solving your customers' problems, not waffling on about how many years you've been in business – they don't care!

7. Just write! If you're not sure where to start or what to say, just write the bits you are sure about. Often when we want to write something, we know key elements of the message but struggle with how to tie it all together. Start with those key messages first and you might be surprised at how easily it falls into place.

Go for it! Whether someone responds to your message or not depends on a multitude of things – timing, design, offer, evidence and of course the words you use to clinch the deal. You don't have to be a trained journalist or marketing guru to write good copy – just get in touch with the truth, get excited and passionate about your product or service, and write from the heart. Use the rules to guide you, write it, edit it and edit it again. But most of all, just write! Like everything else, your writing will improve with practice.

Notes

Notes

Often in our desire to minimize expense and cut corners, we are tempted into "DIY marketing". Yet doing it yourself is fraught with dangers. This chapter will explore the classic mistakes and how to avoid them. That way, if you do decide to embark on "do it yourself", it won't look like a school project and lose you sales!

CHAPTER 8

How to avoid the DIY marketing disasters

Conduct a relevance audit

The first place to start is to audit your existing material. Gather all your printed material together, including your letterhead, leaflets, brochures, flyers, sales letters, annual reports, posters and advertisements. Step into your customer's shoes and consider what image you are portraying through these items.

1. Is there a common look and feel or are they all different? If there is no common style it can be confusing to customers and that isn't good for your business.

2. Is there a common typeface and size? If so, what sort of image do they convey? Typeface (or font) and type size can make a big difference to the "voice" of the message – for example, "First edition comic books available" is very different from **"First edition comic books available."** The first is too stiff and formal for a subject like comic books – it doesn't add to the message.

3. What does the paper quality say about your business? Are you promoting ethical credentials and are your brochures printed on high white virgin paper?

4. Does your printed material look as though it comes from a

124 professional business? Be honest! Are there any spelling mistakes? If there are, you'll lose business because of them.

5. If you had to write down five words that spring to mind when looking at each marketing piece, what would they be?

If you were involved in the creation of this marketing material, or if you feel you are just too close to it to give objective answers yourself, then ask other people. Go to friends and family for their opinion. Ask colleagues from other parts of the business. You could even ask some of your customers. Have them look at the material and tell you their first impressions. What image does the marketing currently project?

This exercise is not about finding out if people do or don't like your marketing; it's about trying to identify how your business is perceived by the outside world, based on the marketing material you have so far produced. This is important for any company, and especially so if you are currently engaged in DIY marketing.

Top 10 clues to spot DIY marketing

1. Your sales letter or brochure is printed on coloured paper.
2. You have used several different typefaces in the marketing material.
3. You have littered your copy with different colours of type.
4. There is no white space on the page – every page is jammed full with words.
5. There is no headline, hook or offer.
6. There are mistakes – usually spelling or grammatical.
7. The image quality is poor and printed to a low resolution. Or it's full of clip-art.
8. The letter is not personalized.
9. The marketing is not targeted .
10. It just looks naff!

Of course not everyone has the budget to hire writers, designers and printers, so if you have to do some in-house marketing, pay particular attention to this chapter so that you can avoid the most common errors.

They say rules are made to be broken, and certainly that applies to marketing. For example, long direct marketing sales letters often break just about every rule in the book! But before you can effectively break a rule you must understand it, so for now let's focus on the basics.

Rookie Buster

Before you can effectively break a rule you must understand it.

Design

You never have a second chance to make a first impression. As a result the design and look of your marketing can make or break your results. If the design of your marketing material screams "home-made", "DIY" or "amateur", then you've lost the opportunity to sell anything. And if the design is poor or unprofessional, your prospective customer won't even read the copy, because they will already have formed an opinion about you within five seconds of seeing your brochure!

Rookie Buster

If the design of your marketing material screams "home-made", "DIY" or "amateur", then you've lost the opportunity to sell anything.

126   Sales and marketing is a process that starts with gaining someone's attention, keeping them interested, highlighting a desire and calling them to action. Design is involved all the way along that process, but it's particularly powerful for getting prospective customers' attention in the first place.

Weak headline and/or weak close

Someone clever once said that if you have ten hours to write an advert, spend nine of them on the headline! No matter how tempting it is to reverse that equation – don't! If you look at the eye-path in the appendix (on page 167) you will see that the headline is one of the first things people notice. If you don't get the reader's attention in those first crucial seconds, then it's all over.

The headline is the advert for your advert. It should shout at a particular target audience and contain compelling benefits. Remember the Four Rs from Chapter 1: Reincarnation, Recognition, Romance and Reward. We are always looking for ways to gain more advantages in life. We want better results, more pleasure, better health, more respect. We want more happiness, more peace of mind, more enjoyment in our jobs, our business and especially our relationships. We want to avoid pain, dissatisfaction, worry, fear, frustration, sadness, poor health and mediocrity in all aspects of our life.

Headlines that offer these things get attention. Your headline must convey an idea and tempt the reader to continue reading. Speak to one reader directly in your ad, regardless of how many people will see it, and use powerful words with announcing qualities. If you are in business to solve a particular problem, talk to people with that exact problem – targeting a small niche audience will always get you more business. Remember that you can always use a different message to target other niche groups too.

Rookie Buster

Your headline must convey an idea and tempt the reader to continue reading.

Once you have the reader's attention, you have to inspire them to action. So your parting words are important: they must explicitly tell the reader what to do to place an order, and remind them of why they need to take action *right now*. Use incentives, closing dates and bonus offers to inspire immediate action. Don't let your communication fizzle out. Look again at the eye-path: you have to make sure that – even if your reader is just scanning the advertisement – key aspects of your offer will jump out. Use the design tips at the end of this chapter to ensure you draw attention to key aspects of the offer, and use bullet points and highlighted words and phrases to get attention. The reader will instinctively look at the end of the letter or advert before the middle, so make sure you reiterate the key benefits of your offer in the PS – and if necessary use a PPS as well.

No testing

Another major error amateurs make is that they don't test their ideas. Testing is particularly important if what you are about to do will require a significant investment. Say for example you decide to run a direct mail campaign, or you are going to introduce a special offer or free gift. Coming up with some ideas at the staff meeting and then making an executive decision on which one you like the best can be suicide. It doesn't matter what you think, or what your friends think, or whether your mother thinks it will work – all that matters is whether or not your customers will respond. And the only way to know that is to test it *before* you order thousands of units or before you roll out a campaign to 10,000 customers.

Don't try to second guess your customers – test your ideas with

128 genuine customers, and monitor the response. When you are testing, never test more than one aspect of the campaign at a time. If for example you wanted to know which headline was strongest out of two or three options, you would only change the headline and nothing else. That way you can be assured that any difference you experience in results is only because of the headline. Aspects of your marketing that you could test are:

- Headline.
- Offer – does a price-based offer outperform a service-based offer?
- Incentives – does one bonus outperform another?
- Timing – does when it was sent or when the advert was placed make a difference?
- Target markets.
- Carrier – does a plain envelope outperform a coloured one, or one with an envelope message?

Rookie Buster

Don't try to second guess your customers – test your ideas with genuine customers, and monitor the response.

Whatever aspect of the marketing you decide to test, make sure you code the response mechanism or the part of the mailing that will be returned with the order from the customer. Otherwise when the results pour in you won't be able to differentiate between the different tests.

Keep testing until you find a marketing piece that is consistently performing well. That now becomes your "control" marketing against which everything else has to be measured – and don't ever change your control unless you can find something that works better. Too often businesses will stumble upon a message that seems to work but then someone will suggest it's time for a change because the customers must be bored. If it's not broke, don't fix it. Instead constantly run new tests against the control to see if you can improve your response.

Rookie Buster

Don't ever change your control unless you can find something that works better.

Although this concept is straightforward and is certainly possible for small business, in practice it's usually only used by those with big budgets. I remember working for an agency in Sydney where we were raising money by direct mail for the Paralympic Games. Often there would be split tests of fifteen or more different variables to find the best performing cell before we rolled the campaign out to over 500,000 households. In the past, that sort of precision cost money!

But not any more. You can now use pay-per-click (PPC) advertising on the internet to help you gauge effectiveness and potential response.

PPC advertising allows you to create campaigns for your product or service using keywords and phrases and to cheaply test between headlines and offers. PPC is a simple, easy and cost-effective way to test your headlines and offers before translating them into offline marketing. See page 170 in the appendix for more details on this.

No follow-up

Apathy is a double-edged sword in marketing. On one hand, the fact that customers never quite get around to returning products, claiming on guarantees or cancelling that monthly membership can be lucrative for business. On the other hand, that same apathy will lose you sales. You send out a mailing or post your catalogue, and your customer may look at it. They may even get quite excited about buying a number of items – and then the phone rings. Or the chip pan catches fire. Or little Sally

130 needs help with her arithmetic homework. Life gets in the way, and the catalogue or the mailer is put aside for another day. Of course that day never comes; before long it's buried under a pile of newspapers and by the time the customer discovers it again the moment has well and truly gone and it gets thrown away. In the meantime, back at HQ you're feeling dejected and unloved because you'd really put some effort in this time. You had found out your target market, polished your USP, used testimonial marketing and risk reversal and created a really compelling offer. So what happened?

You didn't follow up. That's the only reason you didn't get the sale. Yes, it's tough – most people hate doing it – but if you *do* you will make more money. Guaranteed.

You have to follow up. Ideally that would mean a phone call within the first week of the initial contact. Follow-up is especially relevant after direct mail campaigns or sales letters when you have contacted a named person. If you really don't have the capacity to do that, then you should either consider smaller campaigns so that you can, or you could instigate a reminder mailing programme. Send a shorter letter reiterating the marketing message and reminding the potential customer of the original offers. The reminder letter can be sent a week after the original one has landed, followed by another (different) letter a week or so after that. If you are going to use reminder letters. be sure not to remind people who have already ordered (you will really annoy them!), and also make sure you enclose another response coupon and return envelope.

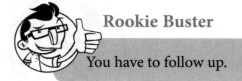

Rookie Buster

You have to follow up.

Telephone follow-up is the best option. It's faster, cheaper, more personal and more dynamic, so you can react to the customer in an appropriate way. And it doesn't have to make your blood run cold. Your customer is a busy person, and if your quick call helps them to

save some time and get what they wanted, then it's a win–win. Have a   131
bonus offer at the ready to help them make a decision straight away
and make sure you ask for the order.

WWW – *woefully weak websites*

We couldn't leave a chapter on DIY disasters without delving into the
world of websites. In the next chapter we'll explore how to create a
good website and make sure it can be found by the search engines. In
the meantime, here's a list of what to avoid.

Top 10 website blunders

1. The use of a "splash screen" or "landing page". This is a first page
   that welcomes the visitor and asks them to click through to the
   home page. Your visitors should be no more than three clicks
   away from everything they need to know, so having a splash page
   is an unnecessary and often irritating extra click. Go straight to
   the home page.
2. Outlandish colours. This is a throwback from the original HTML
   sites, and they look terrible. My personal favourites (not) are the
   bright blue, aqua blue and bright yellow varieties. You may as well
   write "I'm running this business from the spare bedroom" and
   slap it on your home page! Use colour sparingly, and make sure
   that you use web safe colours so you can be assured of a consistent
   result on different machines and browsers.
3. Text offences. Using reversed out text makes it difficult to read,
   especially if the background colour is loud and you've reversed
   your type out in another colour. It can also be difficult to read an
   overly ornate font. If your reader can't read your wacky
   handwriting font, or doesn't have access to that font, then your
   opportunity to communicate is lost. Stick with common, widely
   available fonts, and be consistent across the site.
4. Flashing icons, music or animations rarely add professionalism to

132

a business website (unless of course your business is animation or music based, and the clips demonstrate your work).

5. You have used unnecessary images or large images. Remember that online you have an even shorter time to make an impression, and if a prospective client is waiting for your page to load for longer than a few seconds they will leave.

6. Using frames to split the page into windows may look like a good way to break up text, but search engines hate them. In addition you can't control how they will appear on different browsers.

7. A page counter. There are plenty of ways to find out about visitor traffic without displaying it on the site. Besides, announcing that you've had 87 visitors just isn't very impressive!

8. Scrolling text. If you have something to say, just say it and allow the reader to read at their own pace instead of waiting for the rest of the sentence.

9. "Under construction" notices. Putting the web address on all your printed material and directing people to a page which then announces to the world your poor planning and organizational skills is never wise. Register your domain name and park it until you have built the site, and don't display an "under construction" message.

10. Poor layout. Ideally you want to have all the important copy available to see as soon as the page is opened. Don't make your reader scroll right to finish sentences. Also get to the point before the "crease" of the page – so put all the salient points and attention grabbing headlines before the reader has to scroll down, because the chances of them scrolling down are minimal. And don't centre text or have endless copy – break long copy into sections and make it easy to navigate through the site.

Coach's notes

Seven design tips to make you look like a pro

1. Use white space: leave ample margins and plenty of white space in and around the design. If there is too much copy, tighten the copy through ruthless editing. Don't be tempted to cram it all in.

2. Use only one or two typefaces or fonts. Fonts are divided into serif and sans serif fonts. Serif is when the letters have a little stroke or tail on the letters such as the typeface used for the bulk of this book. Sans serif is a typeface without these little strokes, such as Arial. Sans serif fonts can be good for headlines as they are more "punchy". And serif fonts should be used for body copy as the little strokes make the words easier to read. At least, that's the theory!

3. Don't use too many different type sizes in the design. Have a headline type size and a body copy type size. And don't under any circumstances change the type size in mid-sentence.

4. Create an "eye path" in the design (see the appendix, page 167) so that you lead the reader through the marketing and draw their attention to vital information along the way.

5. Use *word emphasis* sparingly. Instinctively people generally skim read a document first before deciding on its relevance and whether they should read it properly, so you need to pick out *key words and phrases* that relate to the *major benefits*. Don't *overdo* this however, or it starts to look *messy* and *confusing* (see what I *mean*?).

6. Break up the text to make it more accessible to the reader. Bullet points and break out boxes are good for this.

7. Finish pages at interesting sections. Deliberately stop sentences in the middle so the reader is drawn to turn over and keep reading. Never finish a thought on one page or you may lose your reader!

Go for it! Everything you do in your business makes a difference to the way you are perceived by your prospective customers. Whether your marketing materials are accurate or not, if they look amateur, the customer's assumption is that your business is amateur too, and that will lose you sales. Even if your customers appreciate value and you therefore assume (perhaps rightly) that they would not respond to "slick" and expensive marketing, they still want to be sure you know what you're doing. Projecting a professional image doesn't need to cost a fortune – just avoid the common DIY pitfalls outlined in this chapter and you'll be on the right track!

Notes

Presenting a professional online presence is essential. The internet not only gives you access to a global market, but it also levels the playing field of that market, adds credibility to your business and gives you a simple and inexpensive way to keep in touch with your customers. But having a site is only part of the puzzle – this chapter will suggest ways to build your site without breaking the bank, plus essential tips to ensure that your site gets found by the search engines.

CHAPTER 9

Build an effective website and make sure it's found

Build it and they will come

It's difficult to believe that the first webpage was created in 1990. Initially any website was a good website – even those hideous aqua blue HTML ones. But not today!

Open source template software has provided incredible opportunities for people wanting to create their own website without investing thousands. Software such as DotNetNuke (DNN) or Joomla offers a flexible, versatile solution to website creation and management. In days gone by you might notice a spelling mistake on your site and spend several frustrating months trying to get your "webmaster" to make the changes. With open source software, those days are gone – you simply download a template site, choose an appropriate "skin" (design) and start populating it with your content. And because you are in charge, it means that if you do notice a pesky spelling mistake you simply log in to the administration area and make the changes yourself – in seconds. And don't get put off by the word "template", because they offer a remarkable range of flexibility, layout and design.

There is so much to be excited about when it comes to the internet.

138 The things that are possible now are just mind boggling. Advances in understanding and an increase in competition have made everything so much more accessible. If you registered a domain name in 1998 you could have paid £180. Now it can cost about £2.50!

The internet is here to stay, and so the sooner you embrace that, the better for your business. For the first time in history, a small business can truly compete on the global stage with a large multinational. The web has offered opportunities not only in how to reach your market and deliver your product or service, but also in how the actual work is done. In my situation, for example, I have clients all over the world – in Canada, the USA, Australia and the UK. All I need is a website, a broadband connection and a computer. I can call clients using Skype and send work in seconds.

Rookie Buster

The internet is here to stay, and so the sooner you embrace that, the better for your business.

All this freedom and opportunity, however, comes at a price. One of the reasons any site was a good site thirty years ago was that so few people actually had one. Today there are billions of websites. So now the challenge is two-fold – how to create a great site, and how to ensure that the search engines can find it. Even with the impressive advances in internet capabilities it's still remarkable just how few sites are optimized, but that is great news for you!

Creating a successful website is a combination of copy, design, navigation and all the marketing techniques discussed in this book. But even if you get an award-winning designer or a world-class copywriter or the best marketing guru on the planet to help with your site, if none of them knows how to work their magic in the context of the search engines, then you will have wasted time and money.

Search engines such as Google and Yahoo are automated services that send out a software program called a spider (aka bot or crawler) 139 to look at all the sites on the internet. They "crawl" over the sites and insert some of the information they find into the search engine's database – known as its index. So when someone searches for, say, stamp collecting, the search engine doesn't go looking at the internet, it goes to its own index and displays a list of the most relevant pages that match that search term or phrase. You need to know how the search engine defines "relevant", and that's what search engine optimization is all about.

Rookie Buster

You need to know how the search engine defines "relevant", and that's what search engine optimization is all about.

For every search made, the search engine will return two types of results – organic and sponsored links. As the names would suggest, sponsored links are paid for, and organic links are not. Sponsored links usually appear at the top and right hand side of the page, usually against a highlighted background. Both results could be very relevant to your search, the only difference being that one type of business spent time and effort optimizing their site and the other spent money. If you click on a sponsored link, the owner of that site will pay for the privilege of having you visit.

If your website is not optimized, you're losing a valuable opportunity to reach new customers who may never have the opportunity to see your marketing or find your address on a brochure. More and more people are turning to the internet to conduct

140 research and to source products and services they need. Using a search engine is an essential part of that process, so if you are not speaking a language the search engines understand, then you will not be listed. Let's go back to stamp collecting for a moment. At the time of writing, if I type "stamp collecting" into Google, I am faced with a potential 2,190,000 sites about stamp collecting. Most people will look at only the first or second pages of that list – many will not even scroll past the crease of the first page so will only look at four or five results. That means that in the best-case scenario, 2,189,980 sites about stamp collecting have been ignored! Your job is to make sure that you get your website to appear on the first page. Problem is, everyone on the internet is trying to do exactly the same thing!

This chapter is about what you absolutely must do to your website to stand any chance of getting on that first page.

Competitor analysis and keywords

The first step is to create a seed list of words and phrases that you imagine people would type into a search engine if they were looking for the products or services that your business offers. To help in this process, put a few of those search terms into a search engine and see what sites appear at the top of the organic search. Are these companies your competitors? If they are, then you are on the right track. Having a look at competitor sites can give you ideas for new keywords and phrases that you might not have thought of before. Click on "View", then "Source" in your browser, and this will allow you to see what code your competitors have used to create the site. Look to see what keywords they have used for further suggestions.

Also it's important to keep in mind that people don't always use the same words and phrases that businesses use. For example, an electrical appliance manufacturer is unlikely to write copy about their "cheap" products, because it raises questions about quality. Instead they may promote their business as the "budget" alternative, where the customer can get "low cost" electrical goods without sacrificing on quality. The customer, on the other hand, will most probably search for "cheap fridge freezer". Their search is much more specific and straight to the point. Internet searchers rarely get caught up in semantics!

Rookie Buster

Keep in mind that people don't always use the same words and phrases that businesses use.

Once you have the seed list of words and phrases, you need to do further analysis to find out if these are genuinely keywords and phrases that people who are in the market for what you are selling would actually search for. One of the best tools to use is Wordtracker. Wordtracker has the actual results of millions of real searches, so it can let you differentiate between what you think people *might* search on and what they *actually* search on. And it allows you to find unusual or under-served words or phrases that could boost your traffic. Wordtracker also shows you results for all the major search engines and allows you to narrow the search for UK and US searches. There are also a number of free tools available that can give you a starting point, such as the Keyword Tool on Google Adwords. Use these tools to find out what people are really searching for, and get suggestions that you may not have thought of before.

Working out your key words and phrases is important, because you need to ensure they are then strategically placed on your site to increase traffic and listing.

Page title

The page title is the title that appears in the blue bar across the top of the site. So for my own website, *www.wordarchitect.com*, the page title is:

Karen McCreadie|Bestselling Ghostwriter|Copywriter|SEO Webwriter|Fast Turnaround|Word Architect

142   This is one of the first things that the spiders will come across so it needs to be relevant to what people will be searching for. You need to include the most important keywords and phrases that you've identified. For me, that included the type of writing I focus on, my name, business name and a key selling point – fast turnaround.

Rookie Buster

Working out your key words and phrases is important, because you need to ensure they are then strategically placed on your site to increase traffic and listing.

Many sites don't use this space effectively. Depending on the search engine, you can use up to 168 characters in this space. To be on the safe side, it's best to use your most relevant words up front, limit your title to about ten or eleven words and use all the space. Your designer may say that spacing looks nicer, or that the items should be separated by double colons (::) or something equally attractive. Don't do it! The spiders will read these little decorative touches as "stop" characters – that means that the spiders will not crawl your site and will not take anything back to the index and you won't be found. A heavy price for a couple of unsuspecting little colons! Separate your phrases by | and use all the space you've got.

Description

Behind the scenes there is some HTML code that refers to the "Description". It shows up as the little paragraph under the search results to give the reader a bit more detail about that page. In my example opposite you can see the description.

The description is written in the HTML code as <META NAME="DESCRIPTION" CONTENT="Karen McCreadie is an

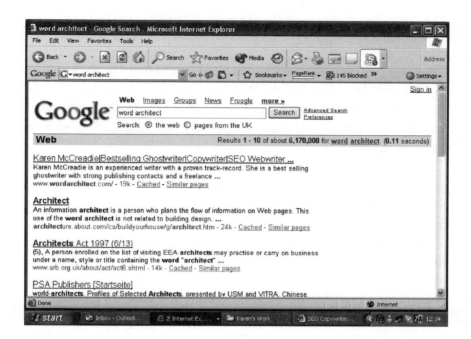

experienced writer with a proven track-record. She is a best selling ghostwriter with strong publishing contacts and a freelance copy-writer assisting clients to deliver a powerful marketing message both on and off-line.">

Again, different search engines allow for different amounts of text, so get your key points in early. If you don't complete this tag in the website design, then the spiders will collect the first copy they come across from the site – and that's not always good. If you want to have control over what appears under your link, then complete this description tag and again make sure you include relevant keywords and phrases. Make every word count.

Rookie Buster

Different search engines allow for different amounts of text, so get your key points in early.

144 ## *Keywords*

Once you have your keywords, you need to add them to the keyword tag in the HTML code. For my site I have used the following keywords. (Notice I've included a number of different ways to spell "ghostwriter". You should think of common misspellings that might relate to your business as well.)

<META NAME="KEYWORDS" CONTENT="hire a ghost writer, ghost write, ghost writer, ghostwriter, copy writer, web site writer, word architect, fast turnaround, seo copywriting, marketing writer, freelance copywriter"

On-line searchers have the attention span of a goldfish, so you have to optimize all of your pages, not just the home page. For example, I offer a Free Relevance Audit on my website. This is a free marketing assessment service that looks at how relevant someone's marketing is to their target audience. Often once we are in business we get so close to what we are doing that we stop seeing it through the eyes of the consumer, and our marketing can reflect that myopia. The relevance audit gives objective feedback on what is working and what is not – whether it's marketing brochures and corporate communications or their website. If someone is looking for "free online marketing advice", for example, it's important that they click through to that specific page, not the home page. So the Free Relevance Audit page is optimized using a specific page title, description tag and keywords.

Rookie Buster

You have to optimize all of your pages, not just the home page.

Page content

In days gone by it was possible to fool the spiders and gain a higher ranking by littering the site with certain words and phrases. However, the copy that actually appeared on those sites often made very little sense to the human being reading it. This can't happen any more, and if you try you risk being blacklisted – besides, what's the point of getting a high ranking, when the information on the home page is gibberish? The searcher is just going to click on past.

Instead, just concentrate on making your site really good! Write relevant copy and meet the needs of your customers. Use all the tips and techniques we've already covered in this book such as testimonials, risk reversal and money-back guarantees. Make sure you include your keywords and phrases naturally in the copy – especially in the first paragraph.

Search engines pay attention to HTML <H1> tags – or headings. They assume that anything in a headline is more important, so try to ensure that your keywords are naturally mentioned in your headings.

Don't get clever – search engines read text not graphics. If your designer has created funky graphic headings, then the search engines can't read them, and you've lost a valuable opportunity for ranking. Make sure your text really is text, not graphics.

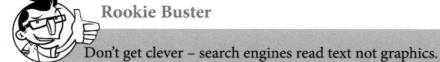

Rookie Buster

Don't get clever – search engines read text not graphics.

Make sure your navigation menu uses keywords where possible, and make everything count. Rather than a menu saying "services" or "catalogue", replace that with "home renovation services" or "relaxation CD catalogue" – whatever it is that you're offering.

It's also worth formatting important text that relates to your keywords. This can be done by putting certain words into bold. To do this, just put <b> before what you want to bold and </b> after it in the HTML code. Some people don't like this, and often in particularly artistic sites, such as a photography site, it's not always appropriate, but it's a personal choice.

Images

If you are using images and graphics, make sure they are relevant to the message or aesthetic and are no bigger than necessary. If the site is slow to load, people will just click past. Make sure that the file names for the images contain your keywords. Even though a human can't see the file name of the image, the spiders can, and they will assess relevance using that information. So ensure your image filenames are related to your business proposition.

Links inside the site

Hyperlink some keywords in the body copy to go to more detail about that subject. For example on your home page you can create links in the body copy, so that if someone is reading there and wants more information on specific aspects of what you do, they can click on the link and go to a dedicated page on that topic without using the navigation menu.

Links

Having links coming into your site is also important for search engines. So if you are a member of an official body and you have an option to have a link from their site into your site, then take it. The more of these you build up the better. But it's important to make sure that they are from credible sources. Don't waste your time or money with link farms.

If you do get the opportunity to create a link into your site, make sure the link actually means something. Say for example you were a nutritionist and had some blurb on a directory or industry body website, and were able to create a link back to your site. Don't make "click here" links; instead make the link text relevant, such as "contact your local nutrition expert" – make that the link. That way the search engine notes that the link content matches your site content and "assumes" that you really are a nutritionist and you have a popular nutritionist site.

Coach's notes

Action steps to assess your site

If you have a website, open it right now and answer the following questions for each page:

1. What appears in the blue page title bar at the very top of the page? It should refer to what you do and include keywords and phrases that are relevant to your business.

2. Is there a heading on the home page? Does it include your keywords and capture the reader's attention?

3. Does the opening paragraph include key words and phrases that prospective searchers may be looking for if they are in the market for your product or service?

4. If you put your business name into Google and it appears in the listings, what description is given about your site? Is this something you have chosen, or has the search engine taken random text from your site?

5. If you click on "View" from the menu and click on "Source" – are there any words and phrases in your keywords tags?

6. If you have graphics, do the images have a name? Have you used the <ALT> tag to give the image a meaning that will be helpful to the search engines?

7. Do you have internal links that help the reader navigate quickly through your site?

If you need to make some alterations to your website, do so immediately so that you can improve your ranking.

Go for it! The beauty of a website is that you can change it whenever you want. You can easily test ideas and copy techniques without reprinting new marketing collaterals such as brochures. But you have to make your website someone's responsibility, otherwise it will slip through the cracks. I've included more information about the open source software packages and where to start in the appendix on page 166, so use this information to create a professional online presence. And remember, a website is always a work in progress – it's never "finished".

Notes

Notes

Marketing is the last thing you can ignore – especially in an economic downturn. If you are experiencing difficulties in your business, the instinctive approach is to batten down the hatches and try to ride it out. Instead you should be using the quiet time to gather the information you need so that you can effectively implement some of the strategies in this book. Good marketing will recession-proof any business.

CHAPTER 10

How to recession-proof your business

When times are tight

Although this chapter is focused on very low cost ideas that can be particularly effective when cash flow is especially tight, in truth they are important strategies that should be implemented regardless of the financial health of your business.

Good marketing takes either time or money. If you don't have buckets of cash to invest, then you must invest the time. The silver lining to an economically gloomy cloud is that, perhaps for the first time, you have it!

Rookie Buster

Good marketing takes either time or money. If you don't have buckets of cash to invest, then you must invest the time.

154 *Customer re-activation campaign*

If someone has bought from you in the past, then you have already surmounted the hurdles and objections that are normally associated with the buying process. So if you've already made a sale to someone – even if it was three years ago – then these people are probably more likely to respond to you again than people with no history.

You will have the information about your past clients somewhere – go find it: collect a list of past clients, including name, address, telephone number, when they last bought from you and what it was they bought from you. If you are concerned that the data may not now be accurate, then you can either use an online business directory or you could contact a list broker and enquire about washing the file against updated census data. Some list brokers may even be able to supply you with new addresses and contacts if someone has moved address in the meantime.

Regardless of how many inactive clients you can track down – test their responsiveness. Take a sample of 30 inactive clients and contact them. Ideally you should call them, simply because you have the opportunity in a phone call to respond immediately to what you hear. Explain that you are contacting them because you notice that they have not purchased from you since such and such a date, and that you are keen to find out if there is a reason they no longer buy from you. Did they maybe have a bad experience with your business? If so, then be prepared to apologize and guarantee that it will never happen again. If they moved because of price, then see if you can match their new deal or improve on it.

So call up your past clients and have a chat. You won't always bring a customer back, and certainly you may even receive a frosty or confused response, but do it anyway. Making the call demonstrates your commitment to customer service in a way that just telling them never will. If you discover there was a problem, at least you have the opportunity to apologize properly and repair the damage. You can explain changes in systems or procedures that have eradicated past problems and find out what you would need to do to get them back on board. If appropriate, you could offer to send them a free sample so they can try you again at no risk. Whatever the response, being in a live, dynamic conversation can greatly improve your chances of bringing them back.

Rookie Buster

Making the call demonstrates your commitment to customer service in a way that telling them never will.

Just think about it yourself – if you have a poor experience with a company, more often than not you can forgive the error if someone holds up their hand and says sorry. I flew to Australia in July 2008 and experienced the worst trip of my life. The airline I used may be the world's favourite airline, but it's not mine! To start with they cancelled my flight out of Newcastle so I missed the connection to Sydney. Despite being assured of a hotel room in London, I spent the first night on the floor in Terminal 5 and then another night in the airport in Dubai. I arrived a day late, no hotel rooms, and to top it all off they lost my luggage – on the way there and (incredibly) on the way back as well. I'm a reasonable person and I understand that bad weather can throw a spanner in the travel works, but what I can't fathom was the attitude of the staff involved. It was appalling. Apart from one exception in Dubai, the crew were rude, dismissive and downright obnoxious. There was not a shred of empathy for the hundreds of inconvenienced travellers and not a hint of genuine remorse.

After making an official complaint I was eventually given an apology and a £150 voucher. I doubt if I will ever fly with them again, but their apology did go a long way in helping to repair some catastrophic damage.

So even if you did really mess up and you find yourself speaking to a very irate customer, say sorry and mean it – you might be surprised what a genuine apology can do to a shattered business relationship.

Rookie Buster

Even if you did really mess up and you find yourself speaking to a very irate customer, say sorry and mean it.

What you will find more often than not is that people didn't stop being your customer intentionally. Apathy moved in, and they just never got around to buying again. If you are armed with offers and special incentives, you may also be surprised at just how easy it is to reactivate that customer. Make sure that you update their contact details and any preferences they have while you're on the phone.

You can expect a minimum of 25 per cent of all those you contact to immediately start buying from you again. Make sure that you get permission from the others to keep them informed of future offers. Collect their email address as this offers a simple and cost-effective way to stay in touch. The irony is that because you contacted them personally (especially if you do so over the phone or in person), then you have demonstrated that you do remember them and are concerned that they no longer buy from you. You have identified them as an individual, not a number, and as such these people often go on to become some of your most loyal and profitable customers.

The other important group you could consider contacting would be the warm list you have of people who have requested information or entered a competition and so on. Trying to convert these people to a sale can be easier that trying to convert people who have no previous knowledge or experience of your business. If these people have at some point been in touch with your business, then reach out to them with a strong enough offer and you may also boost your sales.

Host beneficiary relationships

In difficult times you need to access prospective customers inexpensively. One way to do that is through host beneficiary relationships.

Work out who is already in communication with your target market.   157
Who has already established a strong relationship with these people?

Obviously we are not talking about competitors. You want to iden-tify another business in a non-related, non-competing field that is already speaking to people you would like to talk to as well.

Say for example you are in the carpet retailing and fitting business. You discover from your market and customer analysis that one of your target markets is people building a new home within a 20-mile radius of the store. So who else might already be talking to those people?

- Architects.
- Builders.
- Window suppliers.
- Blinds and curtain suppliers.
- Garden centres.
- Landscape gardeners.
- Outdoor furniture suppliers.
- Lighting suppliers.

Having identified a number of potential types of business that may already be talking to your prospective customers, investigate each one, identify the leading suppliers, approach the one with the best reputa-tion, and ask them to refer their clients to you.

"Why would they do that?" I hear you cry. Because if they remem-ber that their job is not just to do their job well, but also to find out their clients' goals and help them realize those goals, then it makes commercial sense. If the builder realizes that his or her job is not just to build a great house for his client, but also to help that person achieve their dream home, then offering special, relevant and unique discounts to help the client achieve that dream puts the builder ahead of the competition.

The key therefore is to make the host beneficiary business an offer that's too good to refuse. It's best not to offer kick-backs, but instead create special offers that

158 are unique to the business. So for example the builder could give his client a voucher from your carpet business that would entitle that client to one free room carpeted when they carpet the entire house, or free underlay for the stairs when they carpet at least three rooms, or an additional 5 per cent off all carpet. But whatever the offer you come up with, it has to be unique to the host beneficiary so that you are seen to be offering real differentiating value to their customers.

If that builder is smart, he or she will negotiate with a whole range of suppliers, allowing his client to make genuine savings on products and services they are already definitely going to buy as part of their home building project.

Everyone wins. The builder wins because they can use their bonus book and discount vouchers to gain a competitive advantage. All the companies in that booklet of vouchers, such as your carpet business, get access to hot prospects in the market for their product. They may have to sacrifice a little slice of their margin, but it's worth it to gain a new customer. And most importantly, the customer wins because they are making genuine savings. And none of the businesses involved are competing for the same cash.

So put your thinking cap on and work out who is already talking to your target market, and make them an offer they can't refuse. Be sure to make them see the competitive advantage this opportunity can give them.

Rookie Buster

Work out who is already talking to your target market, and make them an offer they can't refuse.

Use incentives for customers

Incentives don't have to cost much money. Look at your current inventory: is there anything left over in old stock that could be bundled up

as an incentive to customers to act now? Think about what resources   159
you already have in the business – in terms of stock and expertise. Is it
possible for you to write a report on your product or service that would
provide customers with vital and valued information?

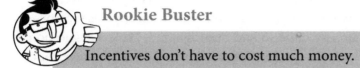

Rookie Buster

Incentives don't have to cost much money.

For example, if you are selling photocopiers to large businesses, you
could include a half day's training to teach staff how to get the most
from the machine or use it most efficiently. Or you could include a
step-by-step report on how to reduce the running costs of the machine
by 20 per cent.

Use incentives for staff

Ask your staff for ideas and suggestions about how to cut costs and
improve efficiencies. When US company International Harvester was
in financial trouble, one of their subsidiaries, Springfield Remanufac-
turing Corporation (SRC), suggested a management buy-out. The new
team took over with no money, no resources, and 119 people all
depending on them to save their jobs and homes.

The head of SRC, Jack Stack, believed in one fundamental premise:
"The best, most efficient, most profitable way to operate a business is
to give everybody in the company a voice in saying how the company
is run and a stake in the financial outcome, good or bad."

As a result of this philosophy SRC grew from strength to strength.
The company is now a collection of 22 separate companies with com-
bined revenue of over $120 million. Many of those new businesses
were created when employees within the business identified weak-
nesses and inefficiencies.

Invite your people to make suggestions about how your business can be improved. These people are at the coal face of your business, and they know the processes inside out because they operate them every day, so it's highly probable that some of them have already noticed the inefficiencies. But unless there is an incentive for them to come forward, or unless the culture is one of constant improvement, it's unlikely they will have stuck their neck out to tell anyone. Or worse still, they have already done so and been ignored. Have a suggestion box to make it easy for people to participate. Review the ideas and reward those who suggest good ideas. Not only will the business save money and become more efficient, but the staff members will feel validated. If this type of collaboration goes on over time, the culture will change and you may find yourself getting some really great ideas from your people. The working environment will improve as the staff feel more appreciated and respected for their contribution, and that will improve their loyalty to the business, their performance and their enjoyment of the work, which in turn helps your business and, most importantly, the customer.

Rookie Buster

Invite your people to make suggestions about how your business can be improved.

Three secret weapons to use in an economic downturn

When business gets tight, the first thing to be cut is the marketing budget and marketing effort. Business traditionally retreats from activity at the worst possible time. In an economic downturn you must do the opposite. Don't let fear dictate your strategy. Besides, if everyone else is retreating from the market, that leaves gaps that a nimble business armed with good customer data can exploit.

Tell it like it is

First of all, don't ignore the economic problems. Everyone knows they are feeling the pinch, so trying to ignore it is just foolish. If there is an elephant in the room – talk about it. You need to gear your message or copywriting towards the fact that there is a recession and wherever possible highlight the benefits you provide within that context. For example, say you sell high-end leather sofas. You might think that people would shy away from your product in an economic downturn, but price alone is rarely a motivation. What people want more than anything else is value, so don't rush to discount your products, but instead draw the customer's attention to the fact that your products are durable. Offer an extended warranty or free Scotchgard treatment with every purchase (usually sold extra for £X). Draw the customer's attention to the value your product offers and how buying a cheaper alternative is a false economy.

Although your advertising should always be truthful, taking this a little further can be extremely powerful. According to Goldstein, Martin and Cialdini's *Yes! 50 secrets from the science of persuasion*, admitting our faults is a powerful tool of influence because it builds trust. Similarly, François, Duc de La Rochefoucauld, the seventeenth-century French writer and moralist, recognized what advertisers are now putting to good use – "We only confess our little faults in order to persuade people that we have no big ones!"

Rookie Buster

Admitting our faults is a powerful tool of influence because it builds trust.

We are assuming of course that the flaws you admit are a) real and b) minor, or c) can be put into a positive context. What makes this strategy even more powerful is when you match the flaw to

162 an associated benefit of that flaw. So for example if you are selling high-end sofas you may want to draw attention to the fact that your products are not the cheapest on the market. If you leave it there you are not really telling the customer anything they don't already know. But if you go on to say, "Yes, our handcrafted Italian leather sofas are expensive, but they are so well made they come with a lifetime guarantee! So you will never have to buy a new sofa again – unless you want to."

By drawing a positive from the flaw, you not only neutralize the problem, but you build trust – and trust sells.

Rookie Buster

By drawing a positive from the flaw, you build trust – and trust sells.

Perceptive contrast

I was in Australia in the summer of 2008 with my family, and the kids wanted to go on the Sydney Harbour jet boat ride. This particular jet boat experience was hailed as the fastest on offer and required that participants removed their shoes and sport an attractive full-length purple poncho! We were obviously going to get wet, much to the kids' delight. So I asked at the kiosk how much it would be for 2 kids and 2

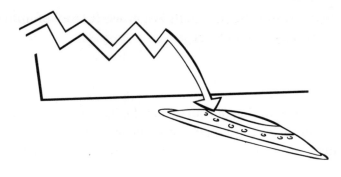

adults. I can't remember the exact amount, but it was well over $250   163
dollars – which was met with a sharp intake of breath and mutterings
on my part. Another chap then appeared at the desk and suggested
that because the boat was nearly full he'd reduce the price to about
$170. I of course accepted. And we all got wet.

Later I was thinking about it and realized I'd just fallen for a technique called "perceptive contrast". Whether knowingly or not, the
salesman had opened the offer so high that I was taken aback. In contrast to that opening offer, $170 seemed reasonable. The fact is that if
he had quoted $170 to start with, I would probably have considered
that a steep price for getting soaked in a jet boat. But in contrast to the
first price I was given, it suddenly seemed like a bargain.

How could you use perceptive contrast in your marketing?

Post-it notes

Social scientist Randy Garner sent out surveys to a random selection
of people asking them to complete and return the study. The survey
was sent with either a) a typed covering letter and a handwritten Post-it
note stuck to the survey, requesting the recipient to complete the
survey; b) a similar handwritten message, but written on the cover
letter; or c) just the survey and cover letter alone. The surveys with a
handwritten Post-it received a 75 per cent response rate compared
with 48 per cent and 36 per cent for (b) and (c) respectively. After
further tests it was concluded that it wasn't just that the Post-it was
brightly coloured and drew the recipient's attention, but that there was
an inherent recognition that the sender had gone to a little extra effort
to get the surveys back. And that extra effort was rewarded (remember
reciprocity here) by the recipient. When Randy added his initials and
"Thank you" to the Post-it notes, the response was even higher. And
what's interesting is the responses also came back quicker and with
more detail when the message was personalized.

Coach's notes

Hierarchy of contact for maximum impact

Personal contact is always best. So, if possible:

- If relevant to your business and the nature of your product, visit your customers. Or if that's not practical…
- Call them up. (The most powerful calls are made from the top of the organization, but if that's not possible, get that person's assistant or PA to do it; and if that's not possible, get your sales manager to do it, or your sales team.) If a relationship exists between the sales person and client get that person to call, or if there were issues between the sales person and client get another person to call. Or if that's not practical…
- Send a personalized letter. But remember, this is not dynamic so you need to follow the rules of good letters and make a compelling offer, etc.

Go for it! Making an extra effort, personalizing your message and making it relevant and compelling to specific target markets works! It might take time and effort, but in a recession that may be all you have.

Appendix

AIDA Formula

The AIDA formula reminds us of the key elements of good marketing and advertising.

A – Attention
You have to get someone's attention. That is why the headline is so important, because you have literally only seconds to grab someone's attention. Specific messages targeting to a niche audience, offering a tangible benefit with a strong promise, will always do this better than generalized statements.

I – Interest
Once you have caught someone's interest with the headline, then you have to maintain that interest and build on whatever desire was targeted in the headline. Don't bore the reader, and keep your message focused on them.

D – Desire

Is your marketing creating a desire for your product? Are you making a compelling offer that is impossible to refuse? The reader must recognize a need and see that you are the solution.

A – Action

You have to tell people what to do. Don't assume they will hunt for your phone number in the small print or go and find an envelope and write out your address. Give them all the information and resources they need to take action immediately. Write your phone number in large numbers, and instead of saying, "Operators are waiting, please call now", say, "If operators are busy, please call again". The second has been proven to lift response because it activates social proof: other people are calling, so it must be OK! Be sure to give people a number of options – phone, mail and email if possible, so that you cater to different communication preferences.

Eye path

Some boffin somewhere discovered that people read advertisements in a particular sequence or path. Your eyes travel across an advert according to the sections in the advert.

1. Pictures

People are instantly drawn toward pictures. A word of warning, however – they have to be relevant to what you're talking about. Sticking an unrelated picture in for the sake of it will only irritate or confuse your potential customers.

2. Headline

Our eyes move next to the headlines. The bad news is that 80 per cent of readers stop at the headlines – this is why it's so important to create a powerful and compelling headline in order to ensure the reader moves on to…

3. The bottom right-hand corner of the page

This is why you often find the name and address of the business there, together with the logo – but you could also add a key benefit.

4. Caption

Interestingly, the captions are not usually read with the picture. But remember, this is the path along which the eye travels around an advert, and it happens in an instant. Readers are twice as likely to read the caption as they are to read the main body text, so you still need to use caption text well.

5. Headings and other graphics

Next people take in the additional headings and the other graphics or illustrations in the marketing. This includes pull-out quotes – pulling key benefits out of the body copy and repeating them outside the copy. (Examples of this can be seen throughout this book.)

6. Body text

This is the least likely to be read, so you can't rely on it to make the sale if you don't already have the headlines, headings, captions and pull-out quotes.

It's important that the elements that are looked at in the order of the eye path work together to build the case for your product or service.

Headline tips

Your headline can ask a question or provoke curiosity, but these techniques are rarely enough on their own to attract attention and keep it. Instead combine these ideas with old-fashioned self-interest. Make bold promises and stand by them. Below is a selection of magic words and tragic words. As the names suggest, the magic words will add power and impact to your headline, and the tragic words will push readers away.

See over the page for the magic words that turn readers on:

- Free
- New
- How to
- Now
- Announcing
- Introducing
- Just arrived
- Improvement

- Revolutionary
- Miracle
- Secret
- Magic
- Offer
- Quick and easy
- Simple
- Truth about

- Bargain
- Limited time
- Last chance
- Save money
- Discover
- Proven
- Guaranteed

They may seem trite but they work – test them for yourself.

Tragic words that turn readers off:

- Buy
- Obligation
- Loss
- Difficult
- Wrong

- Decision
- Deal
- Liability
- Hard
- Death

- Fail
- Cost
- Contract

Open source software

The two most popular open source web application frameworks are DotNetNuke (DNN) and Joomla, and both offer the ideal solution for creating and managing interactive websites. Open source means it is free, which is the icing on the cake for a cost-effective website. They are user friendly and don't require that you understand any programming language or code. The screens you use to populate the site look like common word processing applications. They are extremely versatile, offering basic modules to load text and images to blogs and shopping carts. They are also well supported via online forums and resource portals so you can ask questions, and they allow you to develop your site as you develop your understanding. DNN and Joomla offer cutting-edge capabilities made possible by thousands of independent programmers creating exciting new modules and stunning designs (skins) that are available at a small cost from sites such as www.snow-covered.com (DNN) and www.joomlashowroom.com

Pay-per-click

For more information about pay-per-click and how it can be helpful to your business, visit Google AdWords. There are tutorials and even a program called Jumpstart which provides you with free phone support from a Google expert. That way you can get up and running quickly and have all your questions answered by someone who knows.

Wordtracker (www.wordtracker.com)

Wordtracker allows you to optimize your website content by using the most popular keywords for your product or service, as well as letting you locate little used keywords, generate thousands of relevant keywords to improve organic and PPC search campaigns and research online markets, and find niche opportunities and exploit them before your competitors. It also offers Wordtracker academy, which will teach you how to use the tool effectively using online tutorials. There is also a PDF user's guide available to download.

At the time of writing, if you put Wordtracker into Google and click on "Free keyword suggestion tool" under the Wordtracker entry, you will be shown a link that offers the full version of Wordtracker for 14 days for $1. This will be more than enough time to do your keyword analysis. Even if this offer is no longer available when you check, explore their site, as there is usually a really good offer tucked away somewhere. The site will encourage you to take the free trial, but you have to enter your credit card details and cancel after a week. Wordtracker also understands the power of apathy: they are banking on the fact that you will forget to cancel your credit card payment! Wordtracker is an excellent service, so once you've confirmed its usefulness for yourself with an introductory offer, I would encourage you to subscribe at least once a year to check and update your keywords if necessary.

Index